DISCOVERING YOUR PAST LIVES

The Best Book on Reincarnation You'll Ever Read... in This Lifetime!

GLORIA CHADWICK

D0050387

CB

CONTEMPORARY
BOOKS

A TRIBUNE NEW MEDIA COMPANY

Library of Congress Cataloging-in-Publication Data

Chadwick, Gloria.
   Discovering your past lives / Gloria Chadwick.
   p.   cm.
   ISBN 0-8092-4546-9
   1. Reincarnation.   2. Reincarnation therapy.   I. Title.
BL515.C46   1988
133.9'01'3—dc 19   88-20331
                                                        OIP

This book is dedicated to YOU . . .

to who you are now,
who you have been before,
and who you will become

Contents

Introduction

My interest in reincarnation began one night as I drove past an old cemetery in a town I had never been in before. As I drove past the entrance to the graveyard, I began sobbing hysterically. I knew, without any doubt, that I was buried there. Somehow, I knew my name had been Sarah and the date I had died.

Since it was late at night and I was not particularly fond of exploring graveyards in the dark—not to mention how scared I was—I returned home and thought about my experience all night long. By morning, I had convinced myself that I was crazy. Nevertheless, I went back to the cemetery and walked right over to the grave I felt was mine. The name and dates on the headstone were the same ones I became aware of the night before. As I stood there, looking at my own grave, I began to remember events and emotions that belonged to me when I was someone else.

The experience was so real and so vivid that even my conscious mind couldn't deny it. This experience opened up a new world for me. It was an exciting world of understanding and insight and

1

knowledge about who I was, why I'm here, and the experiences that have shaped and molded me into who I am now. I realized that this experience led to the unfolding of my destiny that I had chosen before my birth into this lifetime.

The knowledge and awareness I have gained, both in this lifetime and in my past lives, are echoes of many different experiences and many voices. The more I learn, the more I become aware of the vast knowledge that is within all of us. This book is my way of sharing the knowledge I have acquired, and is offered to help you remember and understand who you were before, how all of your past lives have led you to who you are now, and how they will influence who you will become.

This book is based on the reincarnation classes I teach, and on the hundreds of past-life regressions I've conducted with students and clients, as well as personal insights gained from past-life recognitions. This book is a *guide* to discovering your past lives, and can help you open doorways into your mind and your soul. It offers one way to open up the doorways that will lead you within, to your inner essence—it is not the only way. Your desire to look within yourself to find your own truth and knowledge will open those doorways for you. As you open your doorways, you'll be reawakening your powerful inner resources, and opening up and expanding your awareness.

The material in this book is presented in a format that allows you to move at your own pace and to absorb the knowledge in your own way. This book is a course into discovering your past lives and opening up the truth and knowledge within yourself. In a class, you can ask questions of the teacher and have points explained that you want to understand more fully. In this book, you'll be answering your own questions and finding the knowledge within yourself. Your answers will guide you to your truth and to your understanding of your past lives.

Some of the information in the book may be a bit difficult to understand at first. There's an important reason and purpose for this. It is my sincere desire to help you learn in the best way possible. Because you're not sitting in my class and can't ask me questions, I've incorporated all the keys and clues you'll need to find the answers within yourself. There are subtle meanings and nuances in the words that may not be apparent on the surface. Only by looking within them will you see and become aware of their true meanings. This book offers you concepts that cannot be fully explained with words, yet these concepts are fully understood when you explore and understand them within yourself and you relate them to your life and your experiences.

Approach reading this book and interpreting the information contained in it by being open and receptive to your feelings and perceptions about it, and to your responses in the meditations, guided visualizations, and opening-up exercises. You may want to skim over the surface of this book the first time through to get a "feel" for the information before you begin to discover your past lives. Read it slowly the second time. Take your time with it and work with your thoughts and feelings about the information and what you experience with it.

The subject of reincarnation is very serious, and is presented in a manner that allows you to discover and explore your past lives in the way that is most appropriate for you. As you open the doorway into discovering your past lives, let your experiences be your teacher. Understanding your past lives is a big step on your journey for knowledge. As you begin to discover your past lives, you may also discover many levels of awareness within yourself.

Many people who have begun to open up their past-life memories have experienced a growing and learning process that led them to become aware of and to develop spiritual aspects of themselves. Some of them started out with doubt and confusion, just as I did, but they searched further within themselves, looking for and finding answers and explanations for their experiences and what it all meant in their lives. Their doubts turned into awareness and insight. Their confusion turned into a clarity that lit their path, and their beginning steps helped them connect with the truth and knowledge within themselves. They experienced a gradual transition into an in-depth self-awareness as they opened up the doorway into their souls, and expanded their horizons by exploring and understanding the true meaning within their experiences.

As you explore and experience your past-life memories, you'll be opening up a world of knowledge within yourself. By discovering your past lives and understanding their effect on your present life, you'll find the meaning in your life and you'll know that you are the master of your fate.

PART I

BEGINNINGS

1

Reincarnation and Its
Relationship to You

As people searched for a way to understand the purpose and meaning of life, they found that all truth was within themselves. They became aware of a special essence they possessed that they termed their soul. They learned, through experiences, that their soul was immortal and that their awareness continued through time. Only the perceptions of this knowledge differed; the truth remained the same. They became aware that death was not the end; it was a new beginning that created a circle of life. They discovered a rhythmic pattern that repeated itself in a rebirth of their soul into a different level of awareness. They found that what they did in one lifetime was reflected in another lifetime.

Reincarnation is the belief in life after death. Your soul is reborn into a new physical body for the purposes of gaining knowledge and for understanding and resolving negative emotions and actions you incurred in previous lifetimes. Through repeated incarnations, you learn karmic lessons and you enjoy the rewards of lessons that were previously learned. As you acquire knowledge and perfect your soul, you attain spiritual union with a higher consciousness.

As you travel the journey from lifetime to lifetime, you encounter experiences in which your actions of previous lives again present themselves. This is known as *karma*, and is commonly referred to as cause and effect. Cause and effect are the same thing as creating your own reality. You create what you experience in every moment of every lifetime. By your thoughts, feelings, and actions, you cause events to occur. When you experience karma, you're experiencing the effect of your previous thoughts, feelings, and actions that you caused and created in your past lives.

In the process of evolving your soul, you become aware of all the actions you've caused. You give yourself the opportunity to experience your karma, and the freedom to choose what you want to do about your karma. You choose whether you'll change and correct what you've done before, if it needs to be corrected, or whether you'll continue the karma into a future lifetime. You also give yourself the opportunity to enjoy and benefit from what you've already learned, and the freedom to increase your knowledge. In your quest for spiritual enlightenment, you become aware that you do, indeed, create your own reality.

Inside the belief in reincarnation is a world of knowledge and self-awareness. To know that you've lived before, and to understand the apparent inequities and injustices of life, brings meaning and purpose to your present life. By accepting responsibility for your attitudes and actions in previous lives, you give yourself the power to make positive changes in your present life, which allows you to learn lessons and balance karma. To know that you have the power to control what happens in your life, and to enjoy the many pleasures and challenges of physical existence, gives you the awareness that you are the master of your fate. By understanding all your experiences, you acquire knowledge and enlightenment, which gives you the awareness of your true spiritual nature.

By discovering who you were before and how your past experiences relate to who you are now, you gain tremendous benefits in terms of understanding your present experiences. The value of remembering your past lives is in applying the knowledge and insights acquired from your past lives to the events, situations, and relationships in your present life.

2

The Process of Remembering Your Past Lives

A philosopher once said, "Learning consists of remembering previously acquired knowledge." Your subconscious mind has a perfect memory and is the storehouse of all your thoughts, feelings, experiences, and accumulated knowledge. Everything you've experienced and become aware of, in every lifetime, is recorded in your mind. Remembering your past lives is a natural process that involves three qualities. Your desire to know; your expectation that you're ready, willing, and able to know; and your belief that you're going to know will open up your memories and allow you to remember your past lives.

All the memories you recall open up for very important reasons that will help you in your present life. They surface to offer you the insights and answers necessary for understanding your feelings about the relationships you're involved in, and they explain your responses to the situations and events that occur in your present life. They help to make you aware of how your present actions and experiences are connected to and caused by past-life events, and they bring you a clear understanding of their influence on your present life. They surface to help you learn life lessons, balance karma, and to educate you in spiritual awareness.

HOW YOUR SUBCONSCIOUS MIND WORKS

In every incarnation, you're born with a new body and a new brain, which serves the purpose of allowing you to function in the physical world. Your subconscious awareness, which contains the knowledge of your soul, is incorporated within your new physical body, with all of your accompanying past-life memories. Your body and brain, and your mind and knowledge, are both similar to a computer. Your body and your conscious brain, known as *Beta*, are the outer covering and circuitry of the computer. Your subconscious mind, known as *Alpha*, is the program disk containing the knowledge that powers the computer. Your body and brain form the shell and the system that receives the inner knowledge of your soul. Your subconscious mind powers and programs the experiences of your present life.

Your brain focuses on concrete ideas and thoughts, and is governed by the conscious characteristics of logic and reasoning. Beta is limited by the amount of information it can receive and process at any one time. Beta is restricted by the physical perspective of information that relates to organizing and analyzing your feelings and experiences. Beta serves the purpose of operating your physical body and experiencing your present incarnation within the framework of the physical dimension.

Your mind focuses on inner truth and knowledge, and centers on receiving and processing both physical and spiritual information. Alpha contains the subconscious secrets of imagery and imagination, intuition and awareness, emotions, dreams, and memories. Alpha operates with an unlimited amount of information in a highly sophisticated framework of awareness. Alpha serves the purposes of acquiring knowledge and helping you to understand all your experiences during your physical incarnation.

Unless the computer is plugged into a power source, it can't operate. Beta and Alpha work together in order for both physical and spiritual awareness to coexist in a physical environment. Beta is like a lamp (body) with a light bulb (brain) that isn't plugged into a power source. Alpha is the energy that contains all the memories of your past lives and plugs into Beta in every lifetime.

Remembering your past lives is like searching the subconscious programming disk. The information is there, but retrieving the file requires the appropriate computer code. Your mind has a unique filtering mechanism that allows you to remember only what is relevant or important to your present life, based on present circumstances. This is because of the vast amount of information acquired in every lifetime.

You may have already discovered your subconscious mind filter. It's similar to the experience of having too many things to do at once, or having too many thoughts running through your mind at the same time. When this occurs, either the computer crashes out (BBB: Beta-Brain Burnout), or your mind filters the information (AAA: Alpha-Awareness Alert), and presents you with the important items you need to be aware of.

Within this filtering mechanism is an intricate filing and retrieval system. You receive so much information on a daily basis that Beta can't absorb and keep it all on a conscious level. It's relegated to the realm of your subconscious, where it's filed in sequence by your feelings about the experience. You only need the proper triggering mechanism to find the appropriate computer code that will bring the information to the surface and show you the pictures of the event in your mind. Most of the time, this computer code consists of associations of similar feelings and events.

Similar emotions or experiences will bring forth past-life memories in which those same emotions or events were experienced. Spontaneous recall of a memory occurs when a present situation or feeling connects with a similar past-life experience. People that you've shared a past life with can also trigger the memory when the feelings you have now are directly affected by past-life emotions. Your responses to the relationship may inspire images of events that occurred before with this individual. The significance of the memory in relation to what you're experiencing now is the activating agent.

Important events are remembered more easily and with greater detail. If there's an important reason for you to remember, then the memory will instantly come to the surface. Being more emotionally involved with the memory also makes it easier to recall, even if the event originally occurred three hundred years ago instead of only last week. Your subconscious mind isn't concerned with time. That's part of Beta's job.

If your past-life memories directly affect an emotional aspect of your life that you're currently involved with, or if they deal with karma you're in the process of balancing, your memories may flood up to the surface and be very dramatic. Your memories will show you images and scenes of past-life events, and you may feel the emotions associated with those events. Your memories will explain how the events and emotions you're experiencing in your present life have their origins in previous lives.

When you first attempt to remember your past lives, or to find information that isn't clearly associated with other events, your mind will begin a search system to reconstruct the events and emotions surrounding the memory in order to bring it to the surface. This is like chiseling stone to get at the core. You'll find all sorts of bits and pieces of memories flying around. When the central memory is located, the emotional aspects come up first, and then the events directly connected to the memory will surface.

THE WAY YOUR
PAST-LIFE MEMORIES SURFACE

When you begin to open up the memories of your past lives, you most often remember first the emotions contained within the memory, rather than the event that originated the emotions. This is because your memories are filed by your feelings. You may see a brief image or fragment of a past-life memory that will cause the associated emotions to surface. A past-life memory may be triggered by a present situation that is similar to a past experience, and you may find yourself responding to the emotions from your past-life memory without recalling the details of the corresponding memory. This can help you understand situations where your feelings are out of context with the present situation.

As you begin to remember your past lives, you may have a sense or a feeling about the memories without seeing them clearly in your mind's eye. You may become aware of a past-life connection without knowing exactly what the connection is. You may become aware of symbols or images that represent something you need to understand before the entire memory surfaces. It's almost as if your memories had a mind of their own. This is partly because Beta and Alpha are learning how to work together in harmony in order for your memories to surface. At first, your past lives may seem like a puzzle with pieces that don't fit together, because Beta and Alpha offer entirely different and separate perspectives about your memories.

You may remember only fragments of the memory that begin to show themselves in fleeting images and flashes of what looks like a past life. Little lights of awareness appear in your mind and tease you with the tip of a memory that disappears the minute you see it clearly, eluding your recognition and understanding. When you begin to see your past-life images, they may zip in and out of your mind with lightning speed. This can prove to be a bit aggravating, especially if you really want to remember your past lives. This occurs when Alpha begins to offer you the memories, and Beta begins to test your sincerity as well as your patience.

When your past-life memories are teetering on the brink between surfacing and being swallowed into oblivion forever, just relax and let them flow up to the surface. This is similar to the feeling when a word is on the tip of your tongue, but you just can't seem to spit it out. When you stop trying to remember the word, and center your attention somewhere else, the word pops into your mind when you least expect it. It surfaces because you let it go with the thought that you'll remember it later. This holds true for past-life memories. Your subconscious mind doesn't like to be rushed or pushed, and can be quite picky about the way you approach opening up your memories.

HOW TO RECOGNIZE
YOUR PAST-LIFE MEMORIES

Until you become familiar with how your subconscious offers your memories to you, and you recognize what a past-life memory feels like and looks like, your past-life memories might seem like they're not really past-life memories. You might tend to think that your mind is playing games with you, and that your imagination is working overtime. Frequently, when your past-life memories are beginning to surface, you're aware of feelings and fragments about the memory that aren't clearly associated with anything in your present life. If your memory has been triggered by a current situation, you may feel emotions that are unrelated to the present situation, and you may become aware of images of past-life pictures.

At first, your past-life images and feelings may be difficult to connect with an experience in your present life. Instead of finding a clear and well-behaved past-life memory that fits into your understanding and falls into your present life perfectly, you may find that your subconscious seems to be trying to hide the real memories. You might even secretly think that your subconscious wants to sabotage your efforts to remember your past lives. This isn't true; it only appears this way when your memories are slow to surface and they show you incomplete pictures. Your subconscious really wants to help you—and will—if you allow it to.

Most past-life memories surface in a quiet, unobtrusive way, but a few are very intense and surface with an emotional impact that bursts into your awareness. When you remember experiences from a past life, and see and feel the images and emotions of the memory, you won't find any type of special signal that goes off in your mind to tell you that the memory is a past-life memory. Your past-life memories are distinguished by how you respond to them. A past-life memory *feels* different from a present-life memory.

Somewhere inside of you, you recognize a past-life memory and you validate it through your feelings about it. When you experience a past-life memory, you *know* it and you *feel* it on a deep level within yourself. This is where trusting your feelings and believing your inner knowledge comes in. Your feelings are the telltale signs of a true past-life memory and pave the way to understanding and insight.

Present-life memories usually feel more familiar at first, and you can place them more exactly with the corresponding feelings after a bit of thought on the matter. Alpha offers you the images and feelings of the present-life memory, and Beta runs them by you in a logical, rational order. Both past and present memories feel real, in their own special way, and the emotions you experience with each are equally valid.

As your memories come up to the surface, you may remember and/or reexperience past-life events and emotions. The depth of your involvement, and how vividly you see and feel the images and emotions of your memories, will determine whether your past lives are remembered or reexperienced. When you're remembering a past-life event, you're viewing the images in your mind and they have a dreamlike quality. You may feel the emotions, but you don't feel the scene. When you're reexperiencing a past-life event, your awareness is completely absorbed in the scene. You're feeling the emotions, *and* you're involved in the events that are occurring. You're hearing, seeing, touching, tasting, and smelling the sights, sounds, and circumstances around you. It feels as if it's happening in the present instead of in the past.

As your memories begin to show themselves, just allow them to surface in their own way. Don't rush them, or force them, or try too hard. This will push them further away from you. Beware of self-imposed limits and restrictions that you place on your memories. Don't become discouraged by expecting earth-shattering revelations and finding small recognitions and little clues to begin with.

Your past-life memories will open up naturally, in the way that is most appropriate for you. By going within yourself and looking into your subconscious mind, you'll discover the doorway into your past lives. The very nature of your subconscious mind is gentle and quiet. Most past-life memories open up in a quiet way, by showing you things you're already aware of, but haven't yet connected to your past lives.

3

How to Find Your Past-Life Memories

Within your subconscious mind are all the memories of your soul. The way to begin to open up your past-life memories is to relax completely. This allows you to tune into your subconscious mind, and in turn allows your subconscious mind to tune into the memories. Relaxation is the art of allowing your physical body to completely let go of all tension, while allowing your conscious mind to free itself from all cares and worries. As you allow a feeling of relaxation to replace tension, all the muscles in your body begin to relax. As your conscious mind becomes calm and quiet, your subconscious mind becomes more aware and you enter an Alpha level, where you're open and receptive to your past-life memories.

ALL ABOUT ALPHA

Being in an Alpha level will feel familiar to you because you've experienced it many times before. You're in an Alpha level when you're thinking quiet thoughts and reflecting on your inner feelings, when you're experiencing a quiet enjoyment of any of the pleasures in your life, or when you're just feeling relaxed and comfortable. You're in Alpha at different times during the day when you're being creative or when you feel inspired. You're in Alpha when you're reading a book or watching a movie and you become involved with the story, or when you're daydreaming or using your imagination. You're in Alpha every night before you go to sleep, and you dream in an Alpha level.

Experiencing an Alpha level of mind has many fringe benefits that aren't directly related to opening up past-life memories. In an Alpha level, you reduce and eliminate stress and fatigue. You let go of Beta characteristics that interfere with being in tune with yourself. You clear out the conscious-mind chatter that distracts and disturbs your attention and awareness. As you become more relaxed, you feel better, both about yourself and about everything around you. You experience very pleasant feelings of well-being and peacefulness. You feel calm and in control of everything you experience. Alpha feels natural and comfortable, and you feel both physically and mentally refreshed. By going within yourself, you develop a more positive attitude, you experience an increase in energy, and you enjoy better health.

In an Alpha level, you enhance your self-image and you build your self-esteem by becoming aware of your positive inner qualities. Being in an Alpha level opens up your inspiration and creativity by allowing you to focus your attention on the positive potentials you have within yourself. When you're in Alpha, you clearly understand your motivations that help you make decisions and achieve desired goals. Alpha gives you the confidence that helps you attain personal success. Being in an Alpha level increases your psychic awareness by opening up your natural powers of intuition and precognition. As you tune into your subconscious mind, you open up your ability to understand your dreams and to be in touch with your feelings about everything in your life. You become aware of your true spiritual nature, and you open up your past-life memories.

MEETING YOUR SUBCONSCIOUS MIND

As you enter an Alpha level, you begin to go within yourself to find your own answers and to allow your past-life memories to surface. Alpha is the true nature of your subconscious mind. Being in an Alpha level feels like a flowing, rhythmic sensation where you're in tune with yourself. Alpha is the key that opens the door to the memories of your past lives. The following meditation will show you how to enter an Alpha level.

Find a comfortable chair to sit in that supports your neck, or a couch where you can stretch out. Begin to relax by breathing deeply. Take a deep breath in and let it out slowly. Focus your attention and your awareness on your breathing for a few moments. Notice how the simple act of breathing begins to relax you, and notice how calm you're beginning to feel. Listen to the sound of your breathing as you breathe in and breathe out, slowly and naturally. Begin to imagine that you're breathing in a feeling of relaxation and a sense of well-being, and that you're breathing out all the tensions and unnecessary thoughts that crowd your conscious mind.

Breathe in the relaxation . . . breathe out the tension. Breathe in the calmness and the quiet . . . breathe out the noise and the disturbances. Breathe in the relaxation and feel it flow naturally through you. Feel all your muscles beginning to relax, as they let go of tension and tightness. Feel the relaxation flowing through your entire body . . . feeling all your muscles relax . . . feeling all your nerves relax . . . feeling every part of your body become totally relaxed and comfortable. Enjoy feeling calm and quiet . . . relaxed and peaceful.

*   *   *   *   *

As you continue to breathe slowly and naturally, feeling relaxed and peaceful, and calm and quiet within yourself, imagine a very beautiful rainbow above you. The rainbow has been formed by an early morning rainfall, and by the sunshine that filters through the clouds. The colors are vibrant and pure . . . a shimmering spec-

trum of colors that blend into one another. It's the most beautiful rainbow you've ever seen. It surrounds you like a perfect dome that touches the sky and the earth. You feel like you could almost reach out and touch the rainbow. You feel like you could breathe in the colors and you could be inside the colors. You feel like you could travel the rainbow from beginning to end, and go into the sky and the universe at the top of the rainbow.

You can feel yourself rising up into the rainbow . . . floating upward . . . rising slowly and naturally into the color red at the bottom of the rainbow. You can feel the color all around you, and as you breathe in the color, you begin to experience the color inside of you. As you absorb the color within your mind, you feel your mind opening up and expanding into the color. You feel your mind becoming more and more aware, and you experience a wonderful feeling of energy as you begin to travel the colors of the rainbow.

You can feel yourself rising up into the color orange in the rainbow. As you breathe in the color, you feel yourself become part of the color. You feel the color inside you and all around you, and the color makes you feel like you're standing on the earth and in the sky at the same time. As you absorb the color within your mind, you experience an exhilarating feeling of freedom. You feel yourself expanding into the rainbow and rising upward into the color yellow.

As you breathe in the color yellow, you can feel the color within your mind. You feel your mind opening up more and more, and you feel yourself becoming more and more aware. You feel like you understand the quality and nature of the rainbow, and you understand the quality and nature of inner truth and knowledge. As you experience the color yellow within your mind, you feel your awareness opening up inside of you . . . expanding and increasing as you open up your mind even more.

You begin to move more easily through the colors now, experiencing the unique energies and vibrations of each color. You flow into the color green, and as you experience the color within your mind, you become more in touch with your inner feelings. You feel the color green with your emotions, and it feels rejuvenating and nourishing. You're aware that the color nourishes your body, as well as your mind. You feel refreshed and healthy, as your body and your mind experience harmony within themselves.

You rise up smoothly into the color blue in the rainbow. As you enter the color, you feel very peaceful and tranquil. You almost feel like your thoughts are words, and that your words are images that spring into action by your feelings. You feel like you can say and see your thoughts at the same time, and that they're really one and the same, with no difference between the thought and the word. You experience a wonderful sense of knowing and understanding that the sky and the earth are really one and the same, with no difference between the universe and you.

As you become aware of this, you find yourself inside the color indigo . . . almost at the top of the rainbow. As you breathe in the color of psychic awareness and true inner knowledge, you feel your mind completely opening up and expanding into ever-widening horizons that go beyond what can be physically seen and touched. You experience your awareness with an understanding and knowledge that goes beyond words and feelings. As you recognize and accept this awareness within yourself, you reach the top of the rainbow.

The color violet at the top of the rainbow inspires a feeling of awe and reverence inside of you. You realize that you've opened up your mind's awareness, and you've allowed yourself to begin to experience your true spiritual nature. You've allowed yourself to begin to experience your soul, and to understand all that is within you.

Above the rainbow, you notice a shimmering white mist. The white mist looks comforting and warm, and feels protective and secure as you wrap it around you, like a cloak of awareness.

* * * * *

As you reenter the rainbow, you feel yourself gradually descending through all the colors you've experienced. You feel yourself blending into the colors of violet, indigo, blue, green, yellow, orange, and red. You find yourself standing on the ground again, looking up at the rainbow above you. You notice the sunshine, as it begins to disperse all the clouds. The sun feels pleasantly warm, and the sunshine is very bright. As you reflect on what you experienced as you felt your mind opening up and becoming more aware, you feel like you've discovered a special treasure within yourself.

By physically relaxing and rising to the top of the rainbow, you enter an Alpha level and your subconscious mind becomes more aware. Alpha is a natural state of mind where you're in touch with yourself on an inner level and where you can allow yourself to meditate. The energies of the colors help you open up your inner knowledge. By going within your subconscious mind, you allow your past-life memories to show themselves to you. You enhance your understanding of how your past-life memories relate to your present life, and why these memories surface at specific points in time.

By allowing your past-life memories to surface, you'll begin to explore the fascinating world of who you were and how all of your experiences have shaped and molded you into who you are now. By looking within yourself, you become aware that you already have all the answers, and you find that true knowledge is within. As you look within yourself, trust the insights and information you become aware of. Give yourself the freedom to explore, the curiosity to learn, the challenge to know, and the power to use what you discover about your past lives.

Being in an Alpha level is a vitally important part of opening up your past-life memories. Every time you enter an Alpha level, with the relaxation and rainbow visualization, you'll find yourself becoming more relaxed and more aware. When you're done with a meditation, feel yourself gradually descending through the colors of the rainbow. This will return you to a Beta level.

You might want to make a recording of this meditation to listen to as you practice relaxing and opening up your subconscious mind. When you feel familiar with entering and being in an Alpha level and you can achieve it quickly and easily, you can shorten the meditation by taking a few deep breaths as you see and feel the colors of the rainbow. Follow your own pace and timing with this meditation.

HOW TO ENCOURAGE YOUR MEMORIES TO SURFACE

While you're in an Alpha level, you can give yourself suggestions for remembering your past lives. When you do this, you're using self-hypnosis. By using self-hypnosis, you rely on yourself to find your own answers. The following suggestions are general in nature and are geared to help you begin to open up your past-life memories. You might want to give yourself these suggestions while you're relaxed and in an Alpha level.

"It's easy for me to remember my past lives."
"I want to know and understand the events and emotions and experiences that occurred in my past lives."
"I can remember everything that is important for me to know and understand about my past lives."
"My past-life memories will help me in my present life."
"My past-life memories will give me insight and understanding."
"My past-life memories will help me understand the origins of events that are occurring now in my life."
"I'm able to remember and understand all the events and emotions that I experienced in my past lives."
"My past-life memories open up naturally, and as they open up, I become aware of them and understand them."

You can formulate your own specific suggestions, based on the information you want to become aware of. Be clear in what you want to remember. Phrase your suggestions in the way you feel most comfortable with, using words that are powerful and positive. Phrases also convey your feelings in an acceptable manner. Your subconscious will respond to words that draw the most vivid images, and to words that inspire action or encourage feelings. (More information on this is given in "Imagery: The Language of Your Mind.") As you give yourself suggestions, phrase them in the first person. Use I and my, rather than you and your. This makes your suggestions more personal and direct.

The way you word and how you feel about the suggestions you give yourself will partly determine the amount of information that surfaces, and will govern the manner in which you remember your past lives. You don't need to be formal with your subconscious mind—just give it a bit of guidance and tell it what you want it to do. Your subconscious has been with you forever and is a familiar friend. When you give yourself clear suggestions, coupled with a positive feeling that you're ready, willing, and able to remember your past lives, you'll find your memories opening up easily and in great detail.

WHAT TO LOOK FOR
WHEN YOUR MEMORIES SURFACE

When your past-life memories begin to surface, there are several important items to look for that will help you recognize past-life images and feelings, and will open up even more details of your memories. These items will place you more directly in the scene and will help you pinpoint specific geographical areas. Details to look for in your memories include:

- how you're dressed (also look at your hands)
- what type of shoe or foot covering is on your feet
- what the landscape or scenery around you looks like
- what the weather or climate is like
- any type of noises, or any kind of smells
- if there's anyone with you, or if you're alone
- what you're doing, how you're feeling, and what your thoughts are
- whether you're male or female, or a child or an adult
- any other visual and sensory details you become aware of

The more you become involved with seeing and feeling your past-life images, the more information you'll become aware of. As you continue to enter an Alpha level to open up and meditate on the images and feelings from your past lives, you'll find that your subconscious mind will become more responsive, and your level of awareness will expand into higher levels of insight and knowledge. As you allow your past-life memories to surface, you'll find that your images will become more clear and detailed, and your awareness and understanding of past-life events and emotions will increase.

4

What to Do with
Your Memories
When You Find Them

As your past-life memories surface, allow yourself to see them and
feel them in the way they offer themselves to you. Resist the
temptation to immediately put them into any type of category or
framework. Many people tend to pick apart the images and
feelings as soon as they appear. If you try to analyze and fit them
into a conscious framework when you're in an Alpha level, you'll
lose the images. This is a conscious pitfall called *Beta blasting*,
where you blow your memories away and smash them into unrec-
ognizable bits. This can occur when your memories first present
themselves and you eagerly pounce on them the minute they
appear. Not everyone falls into this trap. If you do, don't worry. It's
not fatal to the memories and it doesn't last very long.

As your memories surface, allow yourself to experience them
without trying to make any connections with the events in your
present life. The connections will show themselves within your
memories as you allow Alpha to give you the answers. When
you're done with a past-life meditation, write down the images and
feelings. If you're absolutely intent on putting them into a logical

framework, wait until you're in Beta, where you can rationalize and analyze them to your heart's content.

If you doubt the memories that surface, you'll destroy them by dissecting the images and feelings into oblivion. Your memories show themselves in the subconscious images and feelings from your past lives. They're offered to you in an Alpha level, and you can understand them in Alpha. If you try to understand them in Beta, you'll lose the truth in the translation. As you accept your memories in the manner they're offered to you, you allow them to reveal themselves in their proper perspective. With acceptance, you'll understand your memories and become aware of even more information about your past lives.

TRUSTING YOUR FEELINGS

Trust is the cornerstone in building the foundation for your past-life memories to surface. Belief in your ability to open up and recognize your past-life memories, and acceptance of your memories as they surface, are integral and inseparable parts of trust. Past-life memories thrive on your positive belief in yourself, and on your acceptance of the truth within your images and feelings. By trusting your inner knowledge, you always find the truth. Trust turns into truth when trust is accepted and truth is believed.

If you experience doubt at first, accept this as normal. It's just your conscious mind trying to give you a hard time. After all, Beta was the boss for a long time and doesn't like being usurped by Alpha. Beta can resort to nasty tactics like tossing doubt and uncertainty in your way, and will try to play mind games by confusing you and distorting your subconscious images. Beta doesn't like being left out. Actually, this is a good sign and shows you that you're on the right track and well on your way to remembering and understanding your past lives.

If Beta is beginning to sound like the bad guy, then you're already trusting your feelings. Beta does have a few good qualities. It's just that Beta is oriented to seeing only the physical perspective of things, and reacts badly when you begin looking below the surface and beyond the obvious. In trying to regain power, Beta attempts to distract you from remembering your past lives by interfering with your pursuit of true inner knowledge. You can win the Beta battle, armed with trust in yourself and a positive feeling that you *are* going to remember your past lives. Just push Beta gently out of your way. Be nice to Beta, because in the end, Beta will help you put together the puzzle pieces of your past lives.

As you become aware of your past-life memories, trust yourself and your feelings. Trust your own perceptions of what you believe to be true. Believe in yourself and in the memories that feel like past-life memories. As you trust yourself and you follow your feelings, it becomes easier to recognize the true images and scenes from your past lives and to interpret them accurately.

VALIDATING AND VERIFYING YOUR PAST-LIFE MEMORIES

Your feelings about your past lives and the insights you gain into your present life will verify and validate your memories. The best way to verify a past-life memory is by trusting your feelings, and by understanding how your past life relates to your present life. If you'd like concrete proof of your past lives, you can verify them through appropriate channels, by tracing and checking names, dates, and historical data with the information in your memories. The resources you use and the way you validate and verify your past-life memories will be determined by the information you have to begin with. Once you have a starting point, you'll find other avenues to explore. When you verify your memories, you'll be validating something you're already aware of on a subconscious level.

If your past life was recent enough, you may be able to find someone who can fill you in with the facts. Sheila kept seeing a scene of a churchyard in her mind. She saw herself as a little girl, swinging from a tree swing. After that, the image went blank. When she was on a vacation, she drove past that same churchyard. She experienced an incredible feeling of déjà vu. For the next several days, she thought about investigating and verifying her memory, but was afraid of what she might find out.

When she finally summoned the courage to find out more about that lifetime, she went to the church and talked to the priest. She inquired about the history of the church, and specifically asked if anything unusual had ever happened to a little girl there. He recalled having heard that a little girl had been killed in some type of accident, but he didn't know the facts, only hearsay. As Sheila talked to the priest, she remembered even more details about the event, but he was unable to verify them.

Undaunted, Sheila searched through the microfilm of old newspapers in the local library. She found out that forty-three years before, a little girl had broken her neck and died when she fell from the tree swing in the churchyard. Through her research, she was able to verify her past-life memory, and she understood why her subconscious mind had blocked out the trauma until she was ready to remember it.

Doing research at the library can be time-consuming, but it can also prove to be very interesting. The librarians can direct you to reference books and other resources that will help you find the information you need. They're very helpful, especially if you tell them you're working on a research project, or if you tell them you're a writer. If you walk in and announce that you've lived before, they'll probably smile at you in a strange way, but they'll still help you.

If you plan to do research, dress comfortably and develop a liking for sitting on the floor of the library surrounded by thirty or forty reference books. If your past life was really ancient or obscure, you may have to delve through a lot of dusty volumes to find what you're looking for. Carry a lot of change with you for the photocopier. And be prepared for the unexpected. You never know what you'll find at the library.

When you verify your past-life memories, you'll often become aware of even more information about your past life. I had a very enlightening experience while I was researching one of my past lives. My only clue to go on was a word in a now archaic language. I was searching for the meaning of the word, and looking for background information on cultures that had spoken this language.

While I was writing notes from a reference book, I mind-tripped into the past life I was doing research on. I was equally aware of being both my past and present self, and of being in two places at the same time, doing totally different things. I was reexperiencing my past life while I was experiencing my present life. When this happened, I understood the language from my past life, and the events and feelings I reexperienced that day completely opened up my memories of that lifetime.

KEEPING A JOURNAL

The subject of reincarnation is open for your interpretation. This book offers you the opportunity to explore your past lives, and to discover your own truths. I would encourage you to keep a detailed journal of your beliefs, ideas, thoughts, and feelings about your past-life memories and your experiences relating to your past lives. Your journal will build the background and create a foundation for your past-life memories to surface. Your journal will help you better understand both your present life and your past lives, and how they connect with one another.

Throughout this book, you'll find meditations, opening-up exercises, and suggestions for items to include in your journal, as well as ideas you might want to explore on your own. Some of the meditations guide you into your subconscious mind and encourage you to experience a more aware level of mind as a prelude to opening up and exploring your past-life memories. Other meditations guide you into reexperiencing the events and emotions in your past lives by encouraging you to see and feel the images of who you were before and what you experienced in your past lives.

All the meditations are open for you to interpret what you experience and to draw your own conclusions. The meditations offer a beginning point by providing a springboard into your past lives, and encourage you to discover and explore further on your own. The opening-up exercises and ideas offer you the opportunity to acquire even more information about your past lives and encourage you to pursue what is important for you to know.

The exercises and meditations build upon one another, and it's important to do them in the order they're presented. This gives you a firm foundation to stand on and provides you with the necessary stepping stones that will lead you into self-awareness and spiritual knowledge. Keep an open mind as you follow your feelings about what you believe is right for you. Allow your experiences to be your teacher, and to show you the truth within yourself.

As you begin to remember past-life events and emotions, and you begin to see the images of your past lives, write down all the information you become aware of, even if it doesn't make sense at first, or if you're not sure whether it relates to your past lives. Include your feelings about the memories, as well as the images of them. Your feelings are a very important part of your memories. Make notes on the past-life influences and their connections with emotions and events in your present life. As you make entries in your journal, and you connect the clues, you'll find that this will initiate and inspire even more information about your past lives.

The first few pages of your journal may seem like a jumble of images, thoughts, and feelings. What appears to be a mishmash of information and ideas turns into a valuable assortment of keys and clues into your past lives, and represents the opening up of your awareness. The beginning bits and pieces of information tend to become full-blown revelations about your past lives. When you're ready to understand your conglomeration of keys and clues, you'll find that everything fits together and makes perfect sense as you unlock your treasure chest of knowledge and truth.

You might want to begin your journal with your personal beliefs about reincarnation. Define, in depth, what it means to you. Write down how you formed your beliefs, and what influenced them. Get in touch with why you feel the way you do. Your beliefs form the basis of your experiences, and allow you to find your truth. Your beliefs and feelings support and structure your perceptions about what you experience with your past-life memories, and will help you understand both the process and purpose of reincarnation and the immortality of your soul.

Unraveling and understanding your past-life memories is like reading a wonderful mystery novel. Your past lives are filled with interesting and informative characters who will share secrets and clues with you. You'll find fascinating facts and hidden truths. You're the detective, and it's up to you to unearth the clues that will lead you to discovering and remembering your past lives.

Your journal will help you unravel the mystery of your memories by solving the clues necessary to piece together the puzzle of your past lives. When you've completed this guide and your journal, you'll have gathered a tremendous amount of information about your past lives as you open up the knowledge within yourself. Your journal will provide you with a detailed and descriptive narrative about who you were before, and what you've done in your past lives.

5

The Journey Begins

Remembering your past lives is a richly rewarding adventure. Your journey into the past will offer you insights into the present and glimpses into the future. Your journey will lead you on an exploration and discovery of your past lives, and on a quest for inner truth and knowledge. Your search will take you to the heights of awareness, and will show you the essence of your soul. Your journey will open up avenues for you to explore, and will show you paths you've traveled before.

You'll be introduced to your imagination and to the images in your mind, and you'll discover your dreams. Your imagination will reveal your innermost secrets, and will offer you gifts of insight and truth. Your dreams will show you the real world within yourself, and will give you answers to all your questions. You'll take a trip into foreign countries and past-life places, as you visit their civilizations and view their cultures.

Along the way, you'll get to know your inner self, who will be your constant companion and confidant, and who will teach you how to listen to and trust yourself. You'll discover a special place within yourself where you experience harmony and feel the joy of just being who you are. Your inner self will lead you to your true spiritual nature by showing you doorways and giving you the key to knowledge.

You'll reunite with your higher self, who is your oldest, dearest, and most trusted friend. Your higher self will be your guide through most of your past-life memories, and will lead you toward your destiny and the discovery of your purpose. Your higher self will hold your hand as you walk through understanding and balancing your karma. Your higher self will show you the world of truth and knowledge within yourself, and will help you step up into the spiritual realms of awareness, as you reach for enlightenment.

And now it's up to you to walk into the world of self-awareness and spiritual knowledge, and to explore and experience your truth. As you begin to travel the rainbow that journeys into your soul, follow your own path of awareness that leads you to finding the treasure at the end of the rainbow.

PART II

EXPLORATIONS AND EXPERIENCES

6

Déjà Vu:
You've Been Here Before

Déjà vu can provide you with the awareness that you've already remembered pieces from some of your past lives. *Déjà vu* is a feeling of having been somewhere before, or of having experienced something before. When you have a feeling of déjà vu, it feels like something is familiar, but you can't quite recall where you've felt the feeling, and you can't exactly place where you've had the experience. A feeling of déjà vu can reveal a past-life memory, or it can be a reflection of an earlier experience in this lifetime.

One of the first steps in remembering your past lives is to clearly distinguish your past-life memories from your present-life memories. Déjà vu doesn't discriminate between the past and the present as it opens up your memories, and will offer you both past and present images and feelings. It leaves the choice up to you to decide whether the memory is from your present life or from one of your past lives. When you find yourself in a situation that feels familiar, pay special attention to your feelings. Your feelings will connect you with the origin of the memory.

Present-life memories inspired by déjà vu show themselves with a stronger sense of familiarity, and a feeling that the memory is only a thought away from recognition. Past-life memories triggered by déjà vu bring forth a somewhat vague feeling of knowing you've experienced this before, coupled with questions that are prefaced with how, where, why, or when, that offer elusive answers.

As you encounter déjà vu situations that seem reminiscent of a past life, keep in mind that your memories can originate from both your present life and your past lives, and are most often triggered by similarities in the situations. The most typical example of déjà vu is when you find yourself responding to a situation with an uncanny feeling that this has occurred before.

Feelings of déjà vu can originate from a dream you've had, a movie you've seen, a book you've read, or from something someone has described to you or told you about before. When the déjà vu situation occurs, it feels familiar because you were already aware of it, but it was consciously forgotten. Déjà vu can also originate from your subconscious senses of intuition and telepathy, or from a premonition or a precognition, where you have previous psychic knowledge of an event.

Feelings of déjà vu can be indicative of past-life memories, but look deeper within the feeling to discover if it originates from your present life or from a past life. Going through déjà vu feelings with a fine-tooth comb will help you differentiate between a past-life memory and your earlier present memories. This lets Beta know you're serious about opening up your past-life memories, and enlists the aid of Alpha in opening up your inner knowledge.

Look at déjà vu situations you've previously encountered by viewing your experience as being a possible piece of one of your past lives. Déjà vu can be one of those fleeting fragments that first appear when you begin to open up your memories. Beginning with something you've experienced before provides you with a firm footing that helps you determine the direction you take in remembering your past lives. Keep an open mind as you look for the truth. This helps you separate and sort out your feelings. Notice how you feel about the previous déjà vu situation now, and see if you recognize the past in the present.

RECOGNIZING REFLECTIONS OF PAST LIVES

Present situations and feelings can reflect past-life experiences; they can also connect with an earlier experience in this life that originated from a past life. You may have already experienced some of the following situations, which tend to inspire feelings of déjà vu. Your feelings and experiences in any given situation may originate from a past-life memory, or they may be due to a present-life memory. Look within your feelings and reactions to determine whether your response is governed by past-life influences or present-life memories.

While watching a movie or reading a book, you may have identified with one of the characters, or with the scene in the story or movie. You may have had a similar experience earlier in this life that reflects the story, or the story may resemble something you've already seen or read. The theme of the book or movie can also bring a past-life memory to the surface. If the feeling of déjà vu was inspired from a past life, you may become aware of differences between the scenes in the movie or the book and what your experiences were in a past life.

You may have gone on a trip or a vacation to a place you've never been before and known what you were going to see right around the corner. You may have felt drawn to a particular place without really knowing why. You may have gone somewhere for the first time and intuitively felt that you've lived there before, or you may have picked up psychic feelings associated with the place. These recognitions can occur for several reasons. The scenery may be similar to an area where you've lived before, either as a child or in a past life. If you immediately know your way around, you may have lived there in a past life. If you feel drawn to a certain place, it's most often because you experienced happiness there, or because you need to discover and complete something you began there in a previous life.

Something you've never experienced in this lifetime may seem familiar to you, such as the taste or smell of certain foods, or a certain type of music or other sound. This can reveal a past life you've had in a country that is native to that particular food or that kind of music.

You may experience déjà vu in a conversation with someone, where you feel you've had the conversation before. It may have taken place in a previous lifetime, or a similar conversation may have occurred or been overheard earlier in this lifetime, which has now been consciously forgotten.

You may have done something for the first time, and it felt very comfortable and natural, like you've done it before. You may feel an interest in doing certain things, or you may have a natural flair for something. This can represent an ability or a talent that was learned in a past life that is surfacing in the present.

You may have felt an instant attraction or an immediate dislike for someone you've just met. You may have known them in a past life, and your initial feeling tells you whether the relationship was positive or negative. This feeling may also be due to knowing or having known someone similar, and the associations you've formed about that person color your response. This can also occur when you intuitively know whether a person is good or bad, and you respond to the instincts of your first impression.

You may have found yourself in situations where you've become very emotional without knowing why, and your emotions were inappropriate to the situation, or your reaction to a situation was out of character. You may have had feelings you can't quite put your finger on, such as feeling exceptionally good or really bad in some situations, and not completely understanding why you felt that way. When these types of situations or feelings occur, you could be reacting to an emotion contained within a consciously forgotten present-life event, or to a past-life memory that is influencing you, and your feelings and reactions are brought about by the similarities in the situations.

TRACING DÉJÀ VU FEELINGS

You can trace a feeling of déjà vu by focusing on what is occurring in the present, and by following it into the past. By tracing your present déjà vu feeling into the past, you become aware of the origins of your feeling. Beginning with a present feeling or image gives you something specific to follow that helps you unravel the threads of your memory. When you have a déjà vu feeling, notice how you feel about the situation and the way you respond to it. Pay attention to the first thoughts and feelings that pop into your mind. Begin to understand and separate your feelings about the situation to determine if the feeling of déjà vu originates from your present life, or from one of your past lives.

Connect how and why the situation corresponds to your thoughts and feelings about it, and look for a connection earlier in your present life. If you can't find one, then explore the possibilities of how and why a past-life event may have inspired your feelings. This isn't taking a stab in the dark; it's taking a step in the right direction. Subconsciously, you already know exactly where the feeling comes from, and you're opening up the answer by playing with all the possibilities before you go through various steps to find the truth you're already aware of. When you find the origin of your déjà vu feeling, you'll recognize it immediately.

With this as a framework, discover why you're responding the way you are to the present situation by going within yourself and being receptive to images and feelings from your subconscious mind. Enter an Alpha level and focus on the present feeling or image. From your present image or feeling, begin to see the reflection of your past life by allowing images to form that show you scenes from your past life. Trust the images that come to mind, and trust yourself to find the origins of your déjà vu feelings. By exploring and experiencing the feelings and images you become aware of, you'll open up the appropriate past-life memory.

Opening-Up Exercises

Exercise 1. You may have already experienced past-life memories without being aware that many of your present experiences reflected events and emotions from your past lives. Look at the experiences in your present life that could be reflections or influences of events from some of your past lives. Look for any instances where your feelings or reactions seemed inappropriate to the present circumstances.

In your journal, write down a few déjà vu feelings you've

already experienced and what inspired them. Note the initiating experience in this life that triggered your déjà vu feelings, and what your present feelings and reactions are to the situation. This forms the basis to determine whether the déjà vu feeling comes from a past-life memory or a present-life memory.

After you've established the basis for your déjà vu feeling, and if your feeling indicates that it could be a past-life memory, enter an Alpha level and trace the past-life memory by what is occurring in the present. When the associated memory surfaces, it brings insight and understanding into the present situation and your feelings about it. In your journal, write down everything you become aware of in your déjà vu meditation.

Exercise 2. You can actively inspire your past-life memories to surface through déjà vu. By purposely placing yourself in specific situations that encourage feelings of déjà vu, you'll be able to open up many details of your past-life memories. If any of the following situations bring forth a past-life memory, explore it further and make detailed notes in your journal.

- Look through books with pictures of foreign countries that show different cultures and a variety of people. Notice the scenery, the kind of clothes they wear, and their lifestyle. Read stories and descriptions about ancient civilizations. If any of them seem familiar or intrigue you, find out more about the history of the country and the customs of the people who inhabit them.
- Visit museums and look at the artifacts and items on display. You may recognize something you've seen or used in a past life, and images may begin to surface of past-life events connected with those items. The images may inspire past-life feelings, and open up even more details of when you've used these items before, or things you've done or experienced in a past life that are associated with these items.
- Visit landmarks and historical sites. If you feel drawn to a certain area or location, go there and explore. You may

become aware of how it looked in a previous time. When you plan your next vacation, look through the pictures in the travel brochures. The pictures you see may inspire past-life images and feelings. Returning to a place where you've lived before in a past life will further open up your memories of that lifetime.

- If you feel a strong desire to do certain things, become involved in doing them. Delve into and explore your fascination. Find out where it originates and why you feel the way you do. A strong interest in certain things is usually due to a past-life influence. It can represent something you've learned or enjoyed in a past life, or it could be a continuation of something you began in a previous life.

- In addition to the situations described above, originate your own avenues to explore, based on present experiences in your life. Follow your feelings and go with what you feel drawn to pursue.

7

Imagery:
The Language of Your Mind

Imagery and symbolism are the language of your subconscious mind. Your subconscious translates your words and feelings into images, and communicates with you through the pictures it creates from words. Your subconscious responds to your feelings, and to the words and thoughts that create the most vivid and descriptive images. It's been said that a picture is worth a thousand words—but one word can inspire a thousand pictures.

You can see the images of your past lives by looking at them through your mind's eye. You already know how to see subconscious images. You see them every night when you dream, and every time you talk, read, or listen to someone else speak. Words automatically form images and create feelings. Try this out for yourself. Close your eyes and think of a word that describes a person, place, or thing. See what images, feelings, and memories come into your mind. How do you respond to the panorama of pictures and feelings that surface? Notice all the memories connected with the word.

Your subconscious understands your words, thoughts, and feel-

47

ings perfectly, and reflects them in mirror images in your mind. The images and symbols are complete with attached feelings and associated memories, as Alpha opens up a channel of communication with you in its own language. The images you see are Alpha's way of saying "hi" and showing you how it speaks. As you translate and interpret your inner images, you learn to speak the language of your mind by listening to your feelings and paying attention to the pictures you see.

Subconscious images and feelings can reflect past lives, and may rise unbidden to the surface to surprise you with past-life memories. At first, the image and the associated feelings may be a bit difficult to interpret and understand. The image usually represents the opening key into a past-life memory. As you get more in touch with the image and the feelings and recognize the language of your mind, the past-life memory will surface and be completely understood.

SEEING AND SENSING PAST-LIFE IMAGES

You can develop your inner sight and become more aware of the images and feelings of your past lives by becoming involved in the images offered to you by your mind. As you see your subconscious images, you also sense them. Your five physical senses have a major role in helping you to understand and interpret your inner images. Your subconscious mind picks up and records a tremendous amount of information through your senses. By enhancing your senses, your images will become more vivid and clear, and your feelings associated with your images will become more defined.

As you look at something, really see it. Notice all the colors of what you're looking at and seeing, and become aware of other details associated with your visual observations. When you hear something, really listen to it. Become in tune with the sounds you hear. Allow the sounds to form images and to inspire feelings. When you taste something, really savor it. Call your taste buds into action and taste the flavors. When you smell something, breathe it in. Allow the aroma and scent to surround you as you become even more aware of it. As you touch something, really feel it. Be aware of the sensations you feel with your hands, as well as with your emotions.

To become more aware of your inner images, use your five physical senses simultaneously and in connection with one another. Most often, we use them separately and are only aware of one sense at a time. This creates missing pieces of information. As you see, touch, listen, taste, or smell something, allow your mind to form images relating to each of your senses. Then pull all the pieces of the picture together into one picture that tells the complete story in great detail, with vivid and descriptive images and emotions.

By doing this, you'll see the images clearly with your mind's eye, and you'll also sense them within your mind. As your memories surface, the sensory information is intertwined with the images, and you see, touch, hear, taste, and smell the images of your past lives. This places you completely in the picture, and you're involved in experiencing the images. You have a five-dimensional viewpoint, instead of a one-sided perspective.

Opening-Up Exercises

Exercise 1. Your responses to words and phrases create images and feelings that can reveal your past lives. Your past-life images and their associated feelings are connected with words that will bring forth your memories. When you hear a word or a phrase that connects with a past-life memory, your subconscious mind opens that particular image and feeling and brings the memory up to the surface. Free association of words can inspire images and feelings from a past life, or give you insight and understanding into a past life.

- Enter an Alpha level and allow yourself to be open and receptive to the images and feelings from your past lives that the following words and phrases may create. You might find yourself responding to an image by feeling and being in the scene. Notice all the sights, sounds, and smells around you as you see and feel the images in your mind.

In your journal, write down the first thought, image, or feeling you have in response to the word or phrase. If your initial response doesn't seem to make sense, don't stop to analyze it, or try to figure out where it comes from. Stay with the first thought, image, or feeling you become aware of. Move through the words fairly rapidly, as the images and feelings flow instantaneously into your mind.

- Color of red
- Sun/sunrise
- Cornfields
- Blue sky
- Dark clouds and rain; thunder and lightning
- Baby carriage
- Stairsteps
- Parade; troops marching
- Huge crowd gathered outside around a central person, standing on a stage above the crowd, giving a speech
- Quill pen with an inkwell, sitting on top of a desk
- Horse and buggy
- Open field, covered with an unbroken stretch of snow
- Mountainside, covered with trees
- Dark entrance to a cave
- Pyramid
- Bridge
- Desert
- Picture yourself in a mirror—see what you look like
- Piece of paper with writing on it—write down the words you see
- The sound of a phone ringing
- The night sky; stars that are bright and clear

- Center in and focus on the word or phrase that drew the most vivid image and inspired the most intense feelings. Become more in touch with it by writing down all the images, thoughts, and feelings to your initial response. Write down everything that comes to you in the way it comes to you. Don't try to analyze it, or associate it with anything as you write. Just let it flow. When you're done writing, go back and read what you've written. You may be reading about one of your past lives, or you may find definite clues about a past life.

Exercise 2. In your journal, make a list of words and phrases that have a special meaning for you, and do a free association with them. Choose words that you feel will help you open up your past-life memories. Enter an Alpha level and feel the word in your mind. Allow your subconscious to show you images and scenes from your past lives that are connected with your words.

The images you become aware of are keys that will more fully open up your past-life memories. Write down all the images you see in response to your words. Note all your feelings about them, and everything connected with them. After doing the free association, you may discover that all the images and feelings are connected with one particular past life, and you'll find your complete memory opening up in a panorama of pictures.

8

Imagination:
The World of Your Inner Images

Imagination is a powerful resource that will help you open up your memories of past lives. Within your imagination is the world of your inner images, which offers you true insight. Your imagination can accurately show you what your past lives were all about. Through your imagination, you have free reign to express yourself, and to allow your innermost thoughts and feelings to come to the surface and be recognized as the truth.

When your past-life memories first appear, you may feel like you're making them up, or like you're engaging in illusionary imagery that fades when your fantasy ends. If you feel like you're making up imaginary stories about your past lives, it could be due to not yet fully trusting yourself, or perhaps your freedom to play with your thoughts somehow was squelched when you were a child by all the big people in your life. They were taller and bigger than you were, and you may have equated their size and stature with knowledge. Because of this, you might feel that you can only allow yourself to daydream if your conscious mind can deny it when you're through.

The memories that surface are open for your interpretation. When you see them, you could be connecting them with something you're already aware of. If they feel imaginary for this reason, you're recognizing the past-life influence on your present life, and you've got more information than you first thought you had. If you feel like you're creating made-up memories, then discover where your memories originated and what inspired them. As you acquire this understanding, you may find that their basis is firmly rooted in what really happened in your past lives.

INTERPRETATIONS OF IMAGINATION

Your imagination is more real than reality. Imagination is supposed to be something that isn't real, and reality is supposed to be something that is real. There's a widely accepted philosophy that reality is what you can't see, and imagination is what you can see. You may have heard it differently before, but just use your imagination for a few moments and you may begin to see the truth in imagination and the fallacy in fact.

It's a commonly held belief that reality is what you experience in your day-to-day life. Imagination is what you experience in your thoughts. Just suppose that what you imagine on the inside, with your thoughts, turns into what you experience in your day-to-day life. When this occurs, which is real—your previous thoughts that have turned into reality, or the previous reality that has turned into illusion, because it's no longer the reality?

What you believe to be true on the inside is the real part of your reality. Your beliefs about reality determine what you experience in your life. With this premise, perhaps reality is only an illusion, and imagination is the true reality. This concept is worth thinking about, because it can help you determine how you perceive your experiences and how you create your present reality, as well as helping you to open up and accept the past-life memories you feel are true.

The foregoing statements are a crash course in how you perceive and create your own reality. They also relate to how your past-life memories open up and are experienced by you. The underlying basis in what you experience is your belief. Because your beliefs create what you experience, they also influence whether the memories that surface are made-up memories or the real thing. You can feel the difference between fantasies and facts. Trust your feelings.

Your past-life memories and the corresponding images are given to you by your subconscious mind. You already know the truth and you have the answers within. By trusting your inner images, you're able to open another doorway into your past lives. Your imagination can show you what's inside your subconscious mind, without all the judgments and restrictions that belong to conscious denial. By allowing your imagination to open up the real world for you, you'll find that what you originally thought of as fantasy is, in truth, the fact.

REVERIES THAT RECALL PAST LIVES

Using your imagination to reverie about the possibilities of who you might have been, or what you might have done in a past life, is a great way to open up and explore your past-life memories. Reveries can offer you important subconscious truths by uninhibiting your conscious restrictions. Reveries are really daydreams in disguise, and they help you get more in touch with your true inner feelings. When you free up your subconscious mind, and allow it to share its secrets and treasures with you, you've opened the door to your best friend.

Opening-Up Exercises

Exercise 1. You can remember your past lives by employing a reverie about who you might have been before, or who you really were in one of your past lives. This helps you stretch your imagination and expand your awareness. During the reverie, it's important to relax and allow the information to open up and flow naturally. Notice your feelings during your reverie, and whether the reverie feels real or made up. Your feelings help you go within your imagination, and will help you understand the images, thoughts, and feelings you become aware of.

Enter an Alpha level and imagine that you're someone else. Let your thoughts run free, and set your imagination free. Pretend you're someone else. See how he or she is dressed and what he or she is doing. Think that person's thoughts and feel his or her emotions. Let yourself be really free as you flow with the reverie, and see yourself as who you were before. See all the scenes from your past life as you feel your emotions and listen to your thoughts.

What you experience is not a figment of your imagination. It's a bona fide fragment of a past-life memory. In your journal, write down what you experienced in the reverie. Note all your thoughts and feelings when you were someone else. Write down all the images you saw, and note how the information fits in with your present life.

Exercise 2. Open up the truth within your imagination by engaging in several reveries that relate to some of your past lives. Begin with an image or a feeling that fits a past life you feel you might have had. You might want to work with an image or feeling you became aware of in the free association. When you connect with a true past-life memory, you'll be able to feel it. In your journal, make notes on everything you experience.

INSPIRATION AND INTUITION

There are many imaginative ways to remember your past lives. You can creatively express your memories through artistic outlets, such as writing or drawing. Through the creative use of your imagination, you can open up the past. When you tune into a past-life memory, or even a feeling of a past life, and you connect with your related thoughts and emotions about that past life, you become inspired to bring forth elements of the memory that previously escaped your attention.

Your inspiration begins inside you, with something you already know or feel to be true. When you express what's on the inside, you further open up your subconscious mind and allow your inner knowledge to flourish. When you use your imagination and inspiration to remember past lives, you're tuning into your inner truth. As you express your inner knowledge of the truth, you allow your inspiration to flow unimpeded by conscious restrictions.

You can also become aware of your past lives by intuitively recalling and recognizing them. Intuition is knowing something without the conscious use of reasoning. The past-life memory opens itself up when something in your present life triggers the memory, such as a feeling of déjà vu, or an instant recognition of something you've done before. Your intuition also surfaces when you find yourself in a situation that is similar to a past-life experience.

With your intuition, you have a strong and immediate feeling or sense of knowing when something is right, without knowing exactly how you know. This feeling is indicative of the validity of past-life memories. By trusting your intuitive knowledge, the memory will open up to a greater extent and provide you with even more information. When you pay attention to your intuition, you're in tune with your subconscious on an open, honest level, and you're communicating with your inner knowledge, where the truth is free to present itself.

Opening-Up Exercises

Exercise 1. Enter an Alpha level and imagine what you looked like in a past life. Paint the picture in your mind. See yourself as who you were before. In your journal, either draw the picture you saw in your mind, or describe the facial features. Just by studying the picture or description of what you looked like before, you may receive even more information about that past life. Pay particular attention to the eyes and notice the personality that begins to emerge from the self-portrait.

Exercise 2. Use your imagination to write a story about a past life. It doesn't have to be a novel; it can be a short story. Begin by writing about something in your present life that feels like a reflection of a past life. This helps you trace present events to past-life events, and helps you center in on your true feelings. Include lots of details and descriptions. When you're done writing your story, relate it to events and feelings in your present life and note the connections.

You may surprise yourself with your imagination. What appears to be fiction often has its roots in fact. If you're still doubtful about whether your story is real or not, explore where your inspiration for the story originated from. You'll probably find that a past-life memory and your own inner knowledge are responsible for providing the basis of your story.

Exercise 3. Pick a few points from your story that vividly describe an event, or points that brought out some intense emotional feelings for you. Enter an Alpha level and completely open up your imagination and intuition. Set your inspiration and creativity totally free, and allow your memory to provide you with the facts about your past life. In your journal, write down everything you become aware of.

When you're done writing, highlight any references to the present that you recognize. These are the connecting links from the past to the present. What you've written is a detailed account of one of your past lives, complete with connections to the present. You may also find that your story includes several clues for you to open up and explore.

PLAYING WITH YOUR PAST LIVES

While remembering your past lives is serious, you can also have fun with it. Since your imagination originates in your subconscious, it's closer to the memories and can offer them to you in a playful manner. Playing with your imagination can help you discover who you were in a past life and what you've done, based on your present quirks and eccentricities.

Julie classified herself as a neat freak. She would become absolutely hysterical if her rug was dirty; if she saw any stains on the carpeting, she would be depressed for days. She vacuumed every day and rented a carpet shampooer once a week. In a reverie, she became aware of an event in a past life where she was thrown down a well and drowned because she refused to help her brothers clean the carpet. In that lifetime, the carpet had to be cleaned by beating the tapestry with bamboo rods. She's responding to the influence from that past life by making sure her rugs are clean in this life.

Your actions, thoughts, and manner of speech that are unique to you can offer you insights into your past lives. You can look at the possibilities in a light-hearted way that will help you discover the probabilities in a more serious way. The following list offers some thoughts, feelings, and actions you might feel familiar with, or even be guilty of.

- If you ask people how they are by saying, "What's the scoop?", either you were a newspaper reporter in the early 1900s, or you're addicted to ice cream in this lifetime.
- If you say good-bye to people by saying, "Ciao," either you were Italian in your past life, or you're hungry and/or have plans to go out for dinner tonight.
- If you pig out when you're invited to dinner, either you starved to death in a previous life, or you forgot to go grocery shopping this week.
- If your standard opening line when you first meet someone of the opposite sex is, "We were lovers in a past life," either you're telling the truth, or you've found that people really fall for this line.

Opening-Up Exercise

In your journal, write down a list of little quirks, eccentricities, mannerisms, sayings, and idiosyncrasies that are unique to you. Play with them to see where they lead you. Have fun with it and use your imagination. You may discover aspects of your past lives that will provide you with some very interesting insights.

THE SERIOUS STUFF

Playing with your imagination and your thoughts can be a fun way to free your memories. It can reveal important insights and serious aspects about who you were and what you've done in your past lives. Your imagination and sense of humor can open up serious events that might otherwise remain closed. When you shed a little light on the subject, the shadows tend to disappear. You can remove the fear of finding out something that could be painful or traumatic by being a bit irreverent about it. By making light of something that is heavy and burdensome, you can recognize it and let it go, instead of holding onto it forever and allowing it to become a curse that follows you for centuries.

You can become aware of important issues in your past lives that are reflected in the present by making jokes or crazy comments. Ann wanted a serious relationship, but every man she dated rejected her. She joked that she was probably a prostitute in a past life. After she thought about it for a while, she recognized the truth in her statement. By accepting her thoughts, she remembered a past life where she had played with people's feelings. She realized she was experiencing her present difficulty in order to understand what she had done to others and to learn how to respect their feelings.

You may have found yourself in situations where you've thought, "What did I do in a past life to deserve this?" Well . . . what do you think you did to deserve what you got? Keep in mind that karma is always just and fair, and is usually a turnaround of what you've done before. There's an old saying that applies: "Whatever goes around, comes around."

Lisa was abandoned by her boyfriend shortly after the birth of their second son. Feeling desperately sorry for herself, she wondered what she had done to deserve this. She played with the thought that she had probably abandoned her family in a past life. As she realized the truth in her thought, her past-life memory opened up spontaneously. Her boyfriend and her sons were the same souls this time. With the recognition came the understanding that she was accepting responsibility for what she had done before.

You can become aware of serious and sensitive events by allowing them to emerge into the light of recognition and acceptance. Traumatic and painful past-life experiences will surface when they're presented with an accepting environment where they're free to show themselves. You can use pain as a positive resource by reasoning it out to find the truth. This will enable you to see important aspects of your past lives that might otherwise have remained hidden.

Opening-Up Exercise

Choose a situation in your life that is troubling you, or one that seems unfair. Ask yourself what you did to deserve this. Be honest with yourself by letting go of any preconceived ideas, thoughts, feelings, judgments, or rationalizations. Enter an Alpha level and open up your imagination. Allow it to flow with images, thoughts, and feelings of all the possibilities and probabilities of what you might have done or experienced in a past life.

In your journal, write down everything you booomo awarc of. Work with the information you receive about a past life by seeing how it fits into your present life. When you become aware of the truth, it's like a 300-watt light bulb has been turned on, and you can see important parts of your past life you weren't aware of before.

9

Looking in the Present to Find the Past

Your current experiences and feelings often have their origins in past lives. If you've ever wondered why you feel strongly about certain things without having any tangible basis in the present, you can look to the past to find out why. Many present questions and problems have their answers and origins in past lives. Your present experiences are often symbolic of past-life events and emotions. Past-life patterns, choices, and attractions either repeat themselves or are a complete reversal of what you've done before.

Reflections of your past lives are all around you, and are mirrored in your present experiences and feelings. When you look at the present in a new light, you can see through it into the past. Your current lifestyle will show you how the past is continually influencing you, and the framework of your life in general will reveal many clues by giving you an overall and in-depth picture. This helps you understand your present experiences, and helps you connect them to their past-life origins. By looking in the present to uncover clues, you can see into the past.

Underneath the obvious, you'll find clues that reveal your past lives. Carol is a writer in this lifetime. She's always had a great respect for books, and going to the library is the same thing for her as going to church is for devoutly religious people. She spent her childhood absorbed in books. She wrote hundreds of stories and impressed her parents and teachers with her vivid imagination. As a teenager, she preferred books to boys. It's obvious from looking in the present that she was a writer in the past.

Conversations and general clues are a great way to discover your past lives. Betty likes to wear moccasins, and collects silver and turquoise jewelry. Her den is decorated in an Indian motif. She feels she had an incarnation as an Indian, although she wasn't aware of any memories of that lifetime until her ten-year-old daughter came home from school one day and announced that they were studying Indians. She began telling her mother how the Indians treated leather to make it soft. The conversation triggered Betty's memories, and information from her past life began to flow. Betty told her daughter specific details about how she had worked with animal skins to make clothing. Her daughter asked what she looked like when she was an Indian. As Betty described her appearance and the customs of her tribe, she also remembered that her name had been Shana.

Your home and your furniture offer clues about your past lives. Sandy has a fireplace in her home. She felt she absolutely had to have it in order for her home to be cozy and warm. When she got in touch with why she felt so strongly about it, images of a past life opened up, and she saw a home she lived in before that had a fireplace in it. In another lifetime, she remembered living in a cave, and the fire that had kept her safe and warm. Through recognizing the past-life influence, detailed memories about both those lifetimes came to the surface.

Your clothing offers important clues about your past lives. Dave refused to wear a tie to work and felt uncomfortable when he wore anything that fit tightly around his neck. He sometimes has difficulty swallowing and frequently coughs to clear his throat. He has an unconscious habit of pulling collars away from his neck. He thought he might have been hanged in a previous lifetime. In a regression, he realized this was true and became aware of the reasons for the hanging.

Your preference or dislike for certain foods may reveal places you've lived before. When Amy was a child, her parents would often take her out to dinner. Whenever they went into Chinese restaurants, she would become extremely frightened and her throat would close up to the point where she could hardly breathe. At the time, neither she nor her parents could understand her reactions. During a regression, she remembered a poverty-stricken lifetime in China where she was strangled by a snake.

Things you enjoy doing and feel comfortable with give you clues about things you've done before. Carla likes to putz around in her kitchen and makes homemade bread every weekend. She loves the smell of the dough when it's rising, and has been known to eat the whole loaf of bread the minute it comes out of the oven. One time, while making bread, she became aware of what her kitchen looked like in a previous lifetime. She saw images of a wood-burning stove, and could almost smell the stew simmering in the black kettles.

The kind of music and songs you like or dislike can give you clues about past lives. Ever since Frank was a small child, he heard a tune playing in his mind. He hummed the melody to himself almost constantly. One day he heard very similar music on the radio. He called the station to find out the name of the instrumental. He was told the music was a remake of an old tune from the 1800s. He realized that this had been his favorite song in his previous life and that's why he was able to remember the melody.

Sounds you've heard before in past lives can inspire your memories. Whenever Melissa heard the sound of a drumbeat, she felt apprehensive. By focusing in on the sound, she began to see images of a dark-skinned leg adorned with ankle bracelets. She could feel herself dancing barefoot in the sand around an open fire contained within a circle of stones. As she focused in more clearly on these images, she could see other dark-skinned, painted faces. She remembered being part of a culture that killed old and sick members of their tribe. The full memory of the ritual she participated in then came to the surface.

Movies or TV shows may give you clues about previous experiences. When Nancy was watching a movie about a volcano, she became very emotional when the volcano erupted. Scenes of a past life where she died in a volcanic eruption surfaced spontaneously. As she continued watching the movie, she became aware of how the scenes portrayed in the movie were different from what she had experienced. She also understood her recurring nightmares where she was stranded on a small island with red seas and skies all around her.

The books you read offer you clues into time periods and places you've lived before. As a child, Robert was fascinated with stories about the Civil War. After he began reading books on the Civil War, he started having dreams about being a soldier during that time. His parents thought the nightmares were due to all the books he had read on the subject, but he was able to describe scenes vividly and in great detail, and to tell them about experiences he had that weren't in the books he read. These experiences were later verified through research.

Scenes or images you see spontaneously in your mind can show past-life pictures, and they may also reveal past patterns that are continued into the present. Tina has always felt drawn to England. In grade school, she used the Old English spelling of certain words. When she began her writing career, she bought a rolltop desk. When she's working on a book, she keeps the manuscript in a lower-right desk drawer. A short time after she began writing, she started to see images of an old rolltop desk with secret cubbyholes. In a reverie, she remembered a lifetime in England where she was a writer, and had kept her manuscripts in the secret compartment of the lower-right desk drawer.

Your interests, talents, and hobbies reveal clues. In her spare time, Claire loves to do needlepoint. She designs many of her own patterns and with almost every project, knows how to do the stitches without having to read the instructions. As she curls up in a comfortable chair and begins stitching, her thoughts travel to times when she sat by a stone hearth, wrapped in a shawl, doing needlework, and listening to the logs crackle as the fire warmed the cabin.

People you meet who have the same interests or hobbies may be people you've known before. Darlene and Cheryl both make quilts. They met each other at work and immediately became friends. At lunch one day, they began talking about the quilts they were each working on. The conversation inspired déjà vu feelings, and memories of a past life where they were sisters and made quilts together surfaced. As they talked about that lifetime, they were able to provide each other with details that opened up even more information for both of them.

The kind of weather you like or dislike can reveal some of your previous experiences. Adverse weather conditions also offer clues. One night, when Dena was lost, driving through thick and heavy fog, she became aware of images from a past life where she was alone in a boat and was lost in the fog. She remembered being saved by an old fisherman with a scruffy beard. As she saw and felt those images, she realized that the person who rescued her was a friend she knew in this lifetime who also had a beard.

The environment you live in can give you clues. Denise enjoys going barefoot all the time, and summer is her favorite season. She loves plants and trees, and grows her own vegetables. She likes walking in the rain and thunder and lightning storms. She feels close to nature and is protective about animals and trees. She feels she can communicate with them. She's remembered scenes from a past life where she lived on a tropical island and grew her own food. Her culture believed in animal spirits and nature gods who inhabited the clouds and trees.

Strange reactions to certain things or little quirks can reveal many insights into your past lives, and offer you understanding into your present feelings. Peggy always made sure the gas stove was turned off before she left her house. She checked the stove five or six times every day, and would wake up in the middle of the night to go in the kitchen to make sure the stove was turned off. During a past-life regression, she remembered a lifetime where she had died in a gas explosion.

Your personality traits and eccentricities usually have a strong underlying past-life influence. Mary has three hundred pairs of shoes, many of which she's never worn. She loves to go shopping for shoes, and is attracted to shoe salesmen. She goes to the beauty parlor every week and has her feet pedicured. She walks with long, elegant strides. In a reverie, she saw a lifetime in Japan where her feet were bound. When she came of age, and the binds came off, her feet were horribly disfigured and crippled.

Your body and your current health patterns reveal clues about past lives. Birthmarks usually indicate past-life trauma to that particular area. Anything of a serious nature often reflects a karmic connection. Aches and pains that seem to come from nowhere, for no apparent reason, also reflect past-life influences. Bob has always hated horses. To impress his girlfriend, he agreed to go horseback riding. As he was pulling on a pair of boots at the riding stable, he experienced severe back pain. After a visit to the doctor and x-rays, he was assured that there was nothing medically wrong. The pain subsided in a few days. The next time he made plans to go horseback riding, the pain returned. During a past-life regression, he remembered being severely injured when he fell off a horse and was dragged by his boots, which were caught in the stirrup.

Your career often reflects a continuation of a past-life career, or is the direct opposite of what you've done before. Your career choice can give you clues that reveal karma that is being balanced. Lillian was always complaining about her children's education. One day, after listening to her complain about how children were all growing up to be dummies because they weren't being inspired to learn, a friend suggested that perhaps Lillian should become a teacher. The idea appealed to Lillian, who quit complaining and went back to college to obtain her degree in education. She is now a teacher, working with innovative programs that offer children a fun way to learn. In a previous lifetime, she remembered being a slave who was not allowed to go to school. In another lifetime, she prevented her own children from going to school.

Your childhood interests and current hobbies can reveal a talent or an ability that was learned in a past life. Until he retired, James was a carpenter who fashioned intricate designs on the furniture he made. When he wasn't building furniture, he built houses and garages. As a child, he carved pieces of wood into shapes of animals. In a reverie, he saw himself as a barefoot young boy who lived in the mountains. In that lifetime, he whittled small pieces of wood and helped his father build log cabins.

Your family and your choice of friends may be indicative of the kind of friendships or relationships you shared before. The people in your life whom you're close to may have been companions in previous lives. When Melody would touch her small daughter's right hand, her daughter would press her thumb into Melody's hand. Melody thought this was odd, because her mother had done the same thing when Melody held her hand as she was dying. The connection became clear when her daughter was playing with dolls and created situations that Melody had experienced when she was a child.

Current clues offer many insights into what you were like before and what you experienced. They help you understand your present attitudes and emotions, and offer you answers to all the questions you have about your past lives. You can discover many aspects and facets of your past lives by looking in the present and uncovering current clues. When you interpret them, they read like a detailed and descriptive map that leads you directly into your past lives.

CURRENT-CLUES QUESTIONNAIRE

Finding current clues in your life will help you discover events and emotions you experienced in your past lives. The following questionnaire is designed to bring forth memories, and to inspire images and responses that relate to your past lives, based on all your present situations, feelings, and experiences. Your answers to the questions will provide you with clues to open up and explore.

By taking a comprehensive inventory of your present life, you'll find hundreds of clues that reveal detailed information about your past lives. All you have to do is look around you and recognize the signs. It doesn't have to be earth-shattering to get your attention. The small, yet really important clues tend to be overlooked; these are often the ones that reveal the most. The things you're already aware of offer you valuable insights into your past lives.

Go through this questionnaire slowly and thoughtfully. Take your time and write detailed answers to the questions. Really become in touch with your feelings, and explore your answers. If the question requires a yes or no answer, back up your answer with reasons and/or an explanation. The more involved you are in answering the questions, and the more specific your answers are, the more clear your insights and interpretations will be.

You may find that many of your answers will inspire other questions that are relevant to your particular situation or experience. By answering your own questions and taking an in-depth look at your experiences, you'll open up even more details about your past lives. Look at your responses to discover how they reflect a past life, and how your past life is affecting and influencing your present life.

Some of your answers may relate only to your present lifetime. Your responses will help you get in touch with your true feelings, and will give you insights into how you respond to events in your current life. By knowing your feelings and understanding your reactions to everything in your life, you further open up your subconscious mind. This leads to the opening up of memories, whether they involve past lives or your present life. If you're uncertain about your response to a particular question, you can trace your tentative answer by following the present into the past to determine if your response is governed by past or present influences. (See "Tracing Déjà Vu Feelings.") Further explore your feelings to discover if there's a past-life influence.

In answering some of the questions, you may want to center your thoughts into an earlier time. Focus on the image or feeling that represents your past life. This will enable you to reexperience the memory. If you draw a blank on some of the questions, yet feel there's something you want to know more about, use your imagination. Employ a reverie about the question. Set your imagination free and write down everything that comes to you. Trust your feelings about your reveries. You'll be able to determine, by your feelings, if the past-life memory is genuine.

Your responses and feelings may be very powerful, or they may be neutral. You may strongly like or dislike certain images. Get in touch with your feelings and reactions to discover why you feel the way you do. You may also be aware of images or responses that appear to be out of context, or ones that don't seem to make sense. If your answer seems unrelated to your present situation, explore the possibilities of how a past life may have inspired your answer. If your answer seems like it doesn't make sense, you may not yet have all the information you need to form a complete picture about a past life.

To find clear connections for your clues, begin by relating them to the past and present in this lifetime. You may find that your response relates to both the past in this life and also connects with a past-life experience. See if your answer shows a past-life influence. You can be aware of a past-life influence without recalling the specific memory. If your response indicates a past-life influence, then it's highly probable that the influence is a valid clue to a past life. Center in and focus on the past-life image or the present reflection to further open up your memory. Then, note all the similarities and connections between your past life and your present life. When you make the connections between the past and the present, your past-life memory will reveal itself within the connection.

Your answers to all the sections in this questionnaire will give you a great deal of detailed information about your past lives. In your journal, write down all your answers to the questions. Include your feelings, insights, thoughts, and perceptions about each answer. When you interpret your answers, look carefully for past-life influences and images that relate to all aspects of your answers. Your answers will show you the clues and connections to your past lives.

You may find that many of your answers relate to one particular lifetime and show you different facets of your experiences. This forms a biographical sketch, and will fill you in on the overall picture. You might want to list your past lives by countries or time periods. This will help you group together the answers that relate to specific lifetimes. Follow your feelings about which experiences belong in each particular lifetime.

Before you begin, enter an Alpha level and be receptive to recognizing past-life influences. Be open to seeing the images of your past lives that are reflected in your present feelings, situations, and experiences. Trust what you feel are past-life influences, and allow yourself to see through the present images that reveal the past.

Home and Furnishings

Look around your home at your pictures and furnishings. Note any items of furniture that are of a different era. Notice which room in the house you feel most comfortable in, and why you like it the best. How do you feel when you're in the room and how is it decorated? Look at your home objectively, as if you're seeing it for the first time, or as if you're looking at it through different eyes. This gives you a clearer perspective, and enables you to become aware of subconscious feelings and impressions about the atmosphere and the items in your home.

1. Which items of furniture and/or furnishings are your favorite? Why? Which items of furniture and/or furnishings do you dislike? Why?

2. What items of furniture would you like to have in your home that you don't already have? Why? If you were to completely refurnish your home, how would you furnish it, and why would you furnish it that way?

3. What type of house do you live in? What type of house would be a dream house for you? If you could design your own house, what type of house would it be, and how would you decorate it? Why would you design and decorate it in this particular manner?

4. Do you have anything in your home that you've made yourself, such as artwork, afghans, quilts, stitchery, bookcases, or pottery?

5. How is your home or apartment decorated? What kind of pictures or paintings do you have on the wall? Why did you choose them? Is your home carpeted or are the floors bare?

6. Is your furniture mostly modern, or is it reminiscent of a different time period? Are there any items that don't fit in with your main decorating scheme? If so, why did you choose them?

7. Write a description of the type of home you would feel most comfortable and most uncomfortable in. Draw a picture of it, and how it would be furnished. Why would you feel comfortable or uncomfortable in each type of house?

Clothing and Wardrobe

Go through your closet and really notice the type of clothes you have. Look at the clothes you haven't worn for a long time, and note why you're saving them. Notice any articles of clothing that seem different from the rest of your wardrobe. Look at the type of clothes you wear to different places, such as clothes you wear to work and clothes you wear when you go out socially. Notice whether they're similar or different, and how you feel when you wear them. The clothes you feel most comfortable or uncomfortable in will give you important clues.

1. What type of clothes do you like and dislike? Make a list of your clothes, and why you like or dislike them. Notice how you feel when you wear them. What's your favorite outfit, and why is it your favorite?

2. Do you like clothes that are loose and comfortable, or do you prefer clothes that fit tightly? Why? How do you feel when you wear clothes that fit snugly around your neck, such as turtleneck sweaters or shirts with a tight neck opening?

3. Do you like to dress up, or do you prefer casual clothing? Why? How do you feel when you wear formal clothes? How do

you feel when you wear old, comfortable clothes? Do you like clothes that are warm and made of wool, or do you prefer clothes that are light and cool? Why?

4. What kind of jewelry do you like? Why do you like it? How do you feel when you wear it? What type of jewelry or accessories do you wear with certain outfits?

5. Have you ever made any of your clothes, or had clothes made for you? If so, what were the clothes like, and why did you choose that particular style?

6. How do you feel when you go barefoot, or do you always wear shoes? Do you wear shoes or some type of foot covering in your home, or do you go barefoot in your home? Why?

7. What type of clothing do you feel most comfortable and most uncomfortable in? Why do you feel comfortable and uncomfortable in each type of clothing?

Foods and Eating Habits

Notice how you feel when you're in the kitchen preparing food. Notice the kind of dishes and the kind of pots and pans you have. Notice the type of kitchen appliances you have, and the ones you use most often. As you answer the questions about the different type of foods you eat, remember what they taste like. Notice whether any type of food inspires a really strong response. Notice your feelings about the atmosphere surrounding your meals.

1. What types of food do you like and dislike? Why? Is there a certain food that you especially love or hate? Why do you love or hate it? What was your favorite food as a child? Why was it your favorite?

2. Do you eat your meals on the run, or do you enjoy sitting down to a leisurely dinner? How do you feel when you eat by candlelight?

3. What are some of your favorite recipes? Why are they your favorites? Is there a main ingredient that you include with most of the foods you prepare? If so, what is it, and why do you like

it? Do you like spicy foods? If yes, which ones, and why do you like them?

4. Do you eat a lot of the same things, or do you eat many different things? Why? Do you like trying new foods, or do you stay with foods you've eaten before? Are you a picky eater? If yes, why? What were your eating patterns when you were a child?

5. What kinds of food can't you eat? Why can't you eat them? What kinds of food cause you stomach problems when you eat them? Are there any foods you refuse to eat? If so, what are they, and why do you refuse to eat them?

6. When you go out to eat, what type of restaurants do you go to? Do you always order the same thing? What's your favorite restaurant? Why is it your favorite?

7. Are you a good cook? Do you enjoy cooking? Do you like putzing around the kitchen and making things from scratch? Do you invent your own recipes, or do you follow the instructions in the cookbook? On special occasions, what type of food do you prepare?

8. What kind of food makes your mouth water just by thinking about it? Why? How does the smell of certain foods affect you? Name the type of food and your reaction to the aroma.

Music and Songs

Listen to the music in your mind as you're answering the questions. Feel what it sounds like and note your responses. Pay particular attention to the environment you were in when you first heard the music and songs. Notice how you felt when you heard them, and what sort of images they inspired. Notice how you feel about them now.

1. What kind of music do you like and dislike? Why? What's your favorite song? Why is it your favorite? What was your favorite song as a child? Why was it your favorite?

2. How do you respond to instrumental music? The sound of drums? Soft rock? Hard rock? What kind of music makes you

want to dance? Bores you and puts you to sleep? Inspires you? Why?

3. Have you ever taken musical lessons, or do you play a musical instrument? If yes, what instrument have you studied and why did you choose that particular one? Was it difficult or easy for you to learn?

4. Have you ever taken singing lessons? Do you hum to yourself when you're alone? Do you sing in the shower? If yes, what kind of songs or melodies are they?

5. Do you like hearing people sing? If yes, what type of songs do you like to hear? Did anyone sing to you when you were a child? If yes, what song(s) did they sing to you, and why do you remember them? How did the music make you feel?

6. What was the first song you ever heard? Why do you remember it? What sort of images and feelings does it inspire now? What songs do you remember the words to? Why do you remember the words? What do the words mean to you?

7. Have you ever written a song or composed a melody? If yes, what was the song or melody about, and what inspired you to write it?

8. Have you ever heard a tune playing in your mind, but you didn't know where the song came from or where you've heard it before? If yes, describe the tune and how you feel about it.

9. What songs or melodies make you emotional? Do you understand why they inspire strong feelings? List several songs you have a strong response to. Write down how you feel when you hear the song, and what memories and images it brings forth.

Books and Movies

Notice how you feel when you're watching a good movie or a TV show, or when you're reading a good book. Notice if you become involved in, or identify with, what you're watching or reading. Note the images and feelings in your mind in response to the movie or story. Notice the type of books you love to read, and why you like them. See if there's one particular category you enjoy most. Notice how you feel about things relating to books, such as libraries, the smell of printing shops, and how you feel when you open a brand-new book.

1. What kind of books do you like to read? Why? What's your favorite book about? Why is it your favorite, and what does it mean to you? What magazines do you subscribe to? Why do you like them?

2. Do you enjoy reading? If yes, why? If no, why not? Do you read the ending before you read the beginning? Do you read books for studying and learning, or mostly for pleasure? How do you feel when you're in a library or a bookstore?

3. Do you write poetry or prose? If yes, what's it about? Why did you write it? Have you ever written a short story or a novel? If yes, what's it about? Why did you write it?

4. When you read a good book, do you become involved in the story? Do you place yourself in the story and identify with one of the characters? If yes, write a brief synopsis of the book, how you felt when you were reading it, and how you interacted with it.

5. Did you enjoy being read to when you were a child? What stories did you especially like? Why did you like them? What was your favorite book when you were a child? Why was it your favorite, and what made it special for you?

6. Do you like to listen to stories? If yes, why? What kind of stories do you like? Do you enjoy reading or hearing stories that you know aren't true? If yes, why? Do you like human-interest stories? If yes, why? Do you enjoy reading about someone who accomplishes something very important? If yes, why?

7. What movies or TV shows do you enjoy watching? Why do you enjoy them, and how do you feel when you're watching them? Do you relate to them personally? If yes, in what way do you identify with them?

8. What kind of movies or TV shows make you feel angry or

upset? Why? Have you ever become emotionally involved with something you're watching? If yes, what was it about and what made you feel so strongly about it?

9. What's your favorite and least favorite movie or TV show? Pinpoint specific parts of the movie or TV show you like best and least, and write down why you feel that way.

Interests, Talents, and Hobbies

Notice which of your interests, talents, and hobbies you enjoy the most. Describe how you feel when you're participating in them, and what sort of thoughts you have. Note whether your talents were learned in this lifetime, or if they're natural and come easily to you. Notice if you have a flair for doing certain things, or if you feel a strong desire to do something. If you've always wanted to pursue a certain interest, talent, or hobby, your desire could reflect a lifetime where you've enjoyed this before.

1. What are your natural talents and abilities? In what areas do you feel especially creative? Why? What's your favorite activity? Why? What sort of interests, talents, or hobbies do you enjoy? Why do you enjoy them?

2. What do you do in your spare time? What do you like to do when you're alone? What do you like to do with a group of people?

3. When you work on a project or make something, do you have to follow directions? If no, how do you already know how to make it? If yes, do you follow the directions explicitly, or do you alter and improve them to suit your liking? Have you ever seen something that was already made and realized you knew how to make it? If yes, what was it, and how did you know how it was made?

4. Have you ever created or designed something original? If yes, what was it, and why did you make it? What inspired you? How did you feel when you were working on it and when you completed it?

5. Do you collect anything? If yes, what is it, and why do you collect it? What inspired you to begin your collection?

6. Are you inspired by other people? If yes, why, and in what way? Do you admire people who are very creative, or are you jealous of them? Why? Have you ever felt like you could do something better than someone else? If yes, what was it, and why did you feel you could do it better? Have you ever wanted to do something that someone else has already done? If yes, what was it, and why did you want to do it?

7. Do you always complete projects you work on, or do you stop in the middle? Why? Do you have a lot of projects going on, or do you do one thing at a time? Why? Are you working on a project right now? If yes, what is it, and why are you making it?

8. What are you most proud of that you made? Why? What have you enjoyed doing the most? Why did you enjoy it? What are your major accomplishments relating to talents and/or hobbies?

9. What are you interested in that you wish you had more time to do? Why are you interested in it? What sort of hobbies or interests would you like to pursue in the future? Why?

Career and Job

Your career or job and how you feel about it will give you important clues relating to the type of work you may have done in past lives. Your current career may be either a continuation or a reversal of what you've done before. Notice any patterns that emerge relating to your work habits and your attitude toward work. Notice if you're doing what you feel you're meant to be doing, and if your career or job feels right. Pay attention to your feelings about the type of job or career you would love, and why it would make you happy.

1. What type of job or career do you have now? What do you do in your job or career? Do you feel that your job was created for you, or did you just happen upon it by chance? Describe

the circumstances surrounding your employment. Note how you found the job or career you currently have. Note whether you had to struggle to find it, or if it seemed to come to you easily.

2. Are you self-employed? If yes, what do you do, and why do you do it? Who or what inspired you? What events and/or feelings led you to become self-employed?

3. Do you like your job or dislike it? Why? List specific parts of your job that you really like and really dislike. Describe why you feel the way you do. Is your job your choice, or do you feel it's only a way to pay the bills? How do you feel when you're working at your job?

4. Do you enjoy going to work? Is money important to you, or is job satisfaction more important? Why? Do you look forward to what the day will bring? What sort of attitude or feeling do you wake up with in the morning?

5. If you didn't have to work, what would you do with your time? What's your dream about what you want to do with your life? Why do you want to do it, and what inspired your dream? Do you feel you'll accomplish it? If yes, why? If no, why not? What steps have you taken, or would you have to take, to achieve your goal, and how do you feel about them?

6. Do you feel you're meant to be doing what you're doing? If yes, why? If no, why not? If you could have any type of job or career, what would that job or career be? Why would you choose it?

7. What type of work do you feel you might have done in a past life? Do you feel your present job or career is a continuation of something you began in a previous life, or do you feel it's a reversal of what you've done before? If so, why do you feel it's being continued, or reversed, in your present life?

8. Do you feel your job is an interim job that leads to something else? If yes, what does it lead to? Are you studying, taking classes, or involved in some type of learning or training that will lead to another, totally different job or career? If yes, what are you studying, and what does it lead to?

9. Of all the jobs you've had, which job have you enjoyed the most? Why? Which have you disliked the most? Why? Do you do a good job at whatever you do? If yes, why? If no, why not? Are you proud of your accomplishments in your job? List your accomplishments, how you feel about them, and how you achieved them.

10. When you were a child, what did you want to be when you grew up? Why? Who or what inspired you to choose what you wanted to be? Did you have several things you wanted to do, or did you want to do one specific thing? Make a list of things you thought about doing when you grew up. How closely did you follow childhood choices?

11. Do you change jobs frequently? If yes, why? Do you find similar jobs, or are the jobs different from each other? Are you in the process of changing careers? If yes, why, and what type of career are you pursuing?

Health and Body

Notice your health patterns, and how you feel about the quality of your life and your health. Note your feelings about sickness and disease. Your health patterns will reveal many clues about past-life experiences, and may also symbolically reflect your previous attitudes and emotions. Body scars, birthmarks, and psychosomatic pain can reflect a past-life injury or trauma to a particular area, and may reflect karma that is either balanced or in the process of being balanced.

1. What's your best feature? Why are you proud of it, and why do you consider it to be your best feature? Do you like your body? If yes, why? If no, why not? Do you have any physical handicaps or limitations? If yes, what are they, and what caused them? Do you have any physical abilities that are well developed? If yes, what are they, and why did you develop them to perfection?

2. Do you have any birthmarks? If yes, where are they located, and what do they look like? How do you feel about them? Do you have any scars? If yes, where are they located, and what

caused them? What do they look like, and how do you feel about them?

3. Have you ever had surgery? If yes, what type of surgery, and for what reason? Did surgery alleviate the problem, or did the problem return? How did you feel about the surgery and about being in the hospital?

4. Have you ever been involved in any type of accident? If yes, what caused the accident, and how were you hurt? How do you feel about the accident now? If you caused the accident, how do you feel about it, and do you feel it could have been avoided? List several situations where an accident occurred, and what precipitated them.

5. Do you have any health problems? If yes, what are they, and what caused them? How do you feel about your health problems? Do you have a chronic health condition that recurs from time to time? If yes, what is it? How and why did it first appear? What causes it to recur?

6. Do you have to follow a special diet for your health? If yes, why? How do you feel about the diet? Do you have to take pills or other medications for your health? If yes, why? What originated the need for them? Do you have to use any type of machine or mechanical device to help your body function? If yes, what originated the need for it, and how do you feel about it?

7. Do you feel you'll live a long life? If yes, why? If no, why not? How do you feel about the quality of your life? How do you feel about your health in general?

8. How was your health as a child? List any health problems other than the usual childhood illnesses. What caused them, and how did you feel when you were recuperating?

9. Do you wear glasses or contact lenses? If yes, do you wear them all the time, or just some of the time? Why do you have to wear them? Do you wear a hearing aid? If yes, what originated the need for it?

10. Is there any kind of illness or disease that particularly

frightens you? If yes, do you understand the reasons for your fear? Write down why the illness or disease frightens you.

11. Do you have any aches or pains that seem to come from nowhere, for no apparent reason? If yes, what are they, when do you experience them, and what do you feel might cause them? Have you ever had a psychosomatic illness? If yes, what was it? How and why did it originate? Do you know what caused it? And what cured it?

Personality Traits and Characteristics

Answer all the questions honestly. This will give you a true and objective look at yourself. Being clear and open with your answers will help you go within your feelings, and will show you reflections of attitudes and emotions you may have had in past lives that directly affect you in your present life. Many times, your present personality is a turnaround of what it was before. Your current lifestyle will also reveal important clues.

1. In one word, describe your personality. How does that word fit you, and why do you associate your personality with that particular word? How would you describe yourself? How would other people describe you? List several people in your life and how they would describe you. Are the descriptions similar to or different from the way you describe yourself?

2. How do you feel about yourself? Do you like yourself? If yes, why? If no, why not? What do you like best and least about yourself? Why? What's your best and worst personality trait? Why is it your best and worst? What are some of your good qualities? Make a list of them, and why you consider them to be good. Make a list of characteristics you'd like to improve, and why you'd like to improve them.

3. Are you predictable or unpredictable? Why? What makes you that way? Have you ever done anything on impulse without really knowing why? If yes, what was it, and how did it turn out? At a later point in time, did you figure out your reasons for acting on your impulse? Do you sometimes feel that you

don't know what makes you act the way you do? If yes, list several specific instances, and note the initiating circumstances and your reactions to the situation.

4. Do you try to analyze your actions to see where they come from? If yes, why? Do you try to figure other people out? If yes, why? Have you ever been in counseling or therapy? If yes, why? Did you feel the therapy helped you, and what did you find out about yourself?

5. How do you relate to the people in your life? Do you relate the same way to everyone, or to different people in different ways? If you respond differently to certain people, write down why you respond to them the way you do, and how you feel about those people.

6. Are you an introvert or an extrovert? Why? What makes you that way? Do you enjoy being alone, or do you prefer being with other people? Why? Note the situations where you enjoy being alone, and the situations where you enjoy being with other people. Note why you feel the way you do.

7. Do you see the bright side of everything, or do you tend to look on the dark side? Why? What makes you that way? Are you neat, or are you sloppy? Why? What makes you that way? Are you easy to please, or do you have strict rules for yourself? Why? What makes you that way? Are you shy or assertive? Why? What makes you that way? Do you express what you're thinking, or do you keep your thoughts inside? Why? What makes you that way? List several instances that relate to each of the above questions. Notice if there are certain situations that seem to follow a pattern or elicit a certain type of response.

8. Do you cry easily, or do you tend to cover up your true feelings? Why? What makes you that way? What makes you happy and unhappy? Why does it make you feel that way? How do you feel when you cry? What makes you cry? How do you feel when you laugh? What makes you laugh? Do you like the way you laugh? If yes, why? If no, why not?

9. What frightens you? Is there a reason for it? Do you understand where the fear comes from? Write down what you're afraid of, and why you're afraid of it. What's your worst fear? Why is it your worst fear? What makes you afraid of it? Do you have any phobias? If yes, what are they, when do you experience them, and what caused them?

10. Are you proud of everything you've ever done, or are there a few things you'd rather not have anyone know about you? If so, what are they, and why do you want to keep them secret? What's the worst thing you've ever done, and why do you think it's terrible? What caused you to do it?

11. Do you like the way your life is going? If yes, why? If no, why not? List some of the major events in your life, and how they helped to form your present personality. If you could change certain events in your life, what would you change, and why would you change them? What do you feel the outcome would be?

12. If you've experienced some particularly painful or traumatic events, how do you feel about them now? List some of the major changes you've experienced in your life. What did you learn from them and about yourself in going through them? What feelings or emotions do you still have about those experiences?

Friends and Family

Answer the questions by really getting in touch with your true feelings about your friends and your family. Look both emotionally and objectively at yourself, your friends, and your family, and the relationships and interactions with people in your life. Many of the questions relate to important aspects of prebirth choices. Many of your answers will reveal past-life ties with people currently in your life.

Your childhood can also give you many valuable insights. Open up your memories from your childhood and remember how you felt about situations then, without allowing your current feelings to color your responses. Then connect your earlier feelings with your present feelings. When you were a child, notice how you felt when your parents told you to do certain things, or forced you to comply with their wishes. (Being told to go to bed or to use good manners at the dinner table doesn't count.) As an adolescent and an adult, notice how you felt when your friends and family either interfered with your life or encouraged you in the things you wanted to do.

1. Who is your best friend? Why is he or she your best friend? What is it about him or her that attracts you? When you're with your best friend, do you talk a lot, or are you quiet? Can you read each other's thoughts? How did you meet your best friend? Describe the meeting, and how you felt when you first met him or her.

2. Who is your worst enemy? Why is he or she your worst enemy? What did he or she do to you to make you dislike him or her (or vice versa)? How did you meet your worst enemy? Describe the meeting, and how you felt when you first met him or her.

3. Do you have lots of friends, or are you a loner? Why? What makes you that way? Do your friendships and relationships last a long time, or are they short? Why? List several friends you've known for a long time, and why you're friends with them. Why do you feel the friendship has endured? List several people you've known briefly, and why the friendship was short.

4. Who makes you feel happy? Why? Who makes you feel sad? Why? List several people and the situations you're involved in with them that make you feel that way. Who do you feel natural and comfortable with? Why? Have you ever tried to impress people by acting like you're someone that you're not? If yes, why? List several people and the reasons you felt the need to impress them. Note how you felt about them and the situation.

5. How do you feel about authority figures, such as your boss, your parents, your teachers in high school, or your business

associates? Make a list of some authority figures in your life. Note how you feel about them, how you respond to them, and why you feel the way you do.

6. Do you love your family? If yes, why? If no, why not? How do you feel you fit in as a member of your family? Do you feel especially close to one family member, or especially distant from one family member? Why? What makes you feel that way? Write down who you're close to, who you feel distant from, and why you feel that way.

7. What do you like best and least about your family? Why? What makes your family special to you? Do you sometimes wish you had different parents? If yes, why? If no, why are you happy with the parents you have? If you could change certain things about your family, what would you change, and why would you change it?

8. Do you do things with your friends and your family because you feel obligated to, or because you want to? What type of things do you do with your friends and your family? What do you enjoy the most? What do you enjoy the least?

9. What kind of childhood did you have, and how do you feel about your childhood now? What sort of early childhood experiences do you remember clearly? Why do you remember them, and how did they influence you and affect your life?

10. Do you feel your family and/or friends hold you back or encourage you in the things you want to do? List specific situations where you felt your friends and/or your family either interfered with your life or inspired you, and the circumstances surrounding each incident. Has a friend or family member ever said or done anything that changed your life and steered you in a different direction? If yes, what was said or done, and how did it change you?

11. Do you like or dislike your name? If you've changed your name, why did you change it, and how did you choose the new name?

12. List all the people in your life that you feel you might have

known in a previous life. What type of relationship do you have now? What type of relationship do you feel you might have had in a past life?

Sights, Sounds, Scenes, and Situations

For the following questions, become involved in the scenes, and feel the images that the questions evoke. Place your thoughts into a time when you experienced what is described, and notice everything around you. Your first response will more than likely relate to the present, and to what you experienced with each type of weather and situation. Allow your present experiences to lead you into your past experiences. These sights, sounds, scenes, and situations will trigger images and feelings from your past lives, where you've experienced them before, and will open up past-life memories associated with them. List your thoughts, feelings, and experiences in each situation. Your answers to this part of the questionnaire will provide especially vivid responses. How do you feel about:

Seeing a sunrise?
Seeing a sunset?
Clear, blue skies?
A full moon?
Gazing at the stars?
Cloudy, gray days?
Foggy days?
Rainy days?
Snow?
Sunny days?
Windy days?
Humid, sticky weather?
Cold weather?
Warm weather?
Cities?
Farms?
Foreign countries?
Horseback riding?
Flying?

Riding in a car?
Sailing or swimming?
Being at a beach?
Walking in the woods?
Sitting under a tree?
Hearing a waterfall?
The smell of newly cut grass?
The smell of an open fire?
Being in the mountains?
Being in a quiet place?
Being in a noisy place?
Being in a crowded place?
Being in an open meadow?
The scent of flowers?
Thunder and lightning storms?

1. What's your favorite and least favorite kind of weather? Why?
   Do you prefer being inside or outside? Why? What sort of
   activities do you enjoy for each season? Why do you enjoy
   them? Is there one in particular that you enjoy the most?

2. What's your favorite vacation spot? Why is it your favorite?
   How do you feel, and what do you experience when you're
   there? What country or place have you always wanted to visit?
   Why? If you've gone there, how did you feel, and what did you
   experience when you were there?

3. What kind of situations make you feel comfortable and happy?
   What kind of situations make you feel uncomfortable and
   uneasy? Why do they make you feel that way? List several
   specific situations and why you felt the way you did. Notice
   what type of feelings you experienced, and how you feel about
   the situation or circumstance now.

10

Dreams:
The Pictures of Your Past Lives

Dreams are a key to your subconscious mind, and they offer you another doorway into your past-life memories. Dreams bridge the past and the present together, and bring you knowledge and awareness. They reveal insights and answers into your past lives by showing you pictures of how your past affects your present. Dreams offer you everything you want to know, but were afraid to ask; they'll even tell you things you don't want to know, but did have the courage to ask.

Dreams contain all the knowledge in the world and in the universe. They're an authoritative and expert guide into the realms of spiritual mysteries and mastery. Dreams show you the magical and mystical world within yourself, and provide you with knowledge and awareness that helps you in every avenue and aspect of your life. As you explore and experience your dreams, you'll discover how your subconscious mind shows you your past lives, and you'll open up your spiritual awareness.

Sleep serves a dual purpose. It allows you to rest your body by tuning out your physical nature. Sleep allows your subconscious mind to become active by tuning into your spiritual nature. As you sleep, you center in and focus on spiritual energies. You connect with your subconscious self and you plug into your true spiritual nature. This balance is vital and is what enables your soul to exist in a physical body.

Your subconscious mind is on a different wavelength than your conscious mind. Your spiritual self and your physical self are as different as night and day, and they operate on different levels of awareness and energy. As you dream, you tune into your inner knowledge and open up your spiritual nature. In your dreams, your spiritual awareness and your past-life memories have free reign to express themselves.

DISCOVERING YOUR PAST LIVES
THROUGH YOUR DREAMS

Your past lives will show themselves through your dreams. Your dreams will accurately portray events and emotions from your past lives, and will give you insights into the memory and information about why the memory is surfacing in your present life. Some of your dreams will offer you clear images of past-life events; others will give you clouded images that are shrouded in symbology. Your dreams will show you scenes from your past lives, as well as giving you an understanding of them. Your dreams are an experience that offer you an in-depth view of how you perceive your past lives.

The first type of past-life dreams are easiest to recognize because the images and events in the dream are shown in the appropriate time frame. The dream offers you insights into a past life by showing you very clear and literal images of who you were before and what you experienced. The dream images show themselves in a flowing type of movement, hitting the highlights of past-life scenes that relate directly to your present life. These dreams interpret themselves by showing you the relationship between what you're currently experiencing and what you experienced in your past life.

The second type of past-life dreams provides you with feelings and fragments of past-life pictures. The dreams relate specifically to learning a karmic lesson, and often include people you're currently involved with whom you experienced a past life with. The dream replays events and emotions you've experienced in past lives that are now affecting you, and symbolically portrays the karma that requires balancing. The dreams may recur, showing you different images with the same message, until you've understood and balanced the past-life event or emotion.

This type of dream can be a bit difficult to recognize, because it shows you present situations that are similar to past-life experiences, and you dream about the past in a present framework of time. The dream images may appear to be totally unrelated to your past life. As you recognize the reflection of past-life events and emotions, the imagery and content of the dream changes to reveal past-life pictures.

As you become involved in your dream by symbolically balancing the karma you become aware of in the dream and simultaneously balancing the karma in your present life, the dreams may begin to show themselves in lucid form. In a lucid dream, you're consciously aware of the dream as you're dreaming it, and you actively participate in the dream as you observe it. (Your spiritual awareness begins to blend and harmonize with your physical awareness, and this is what causes lucid dreams of this type.)

Lucid dreaming opens up a channel of communication between your conscious mind and your subconscious mind. Once the dream opens up into a lucid dream, you can continue with lucid dreaming to discover all that you want to know. This gives you a great deal of clear information about past events and emotions and the connections to corresponding present events and emotions. You can program yourself to have lucid dreams about your past lives. Do this by telling your subconscious mind to connect with your conscious mind while you're still sleeping. (This may take a bit of practice.)

The third type of past-life dreams occurs after you've learned a karmic lesson or balanced karma. These dreams confirm the lesson that was learned or the karma that was balanced. The dream imagery is symbolic and literal at the same time, and the pictures are shown in images you're already familiar with. The dream provides you with the awareness of your accomplishment and shows you the rewards you've earned. After having one of these dreams, you wake up with a feeling of spiritual nourishment and inner peace.

Another version of this dream verifies memories you may already be aware of. It shows you how to understand your past life better, as well as offering you ways to complete your karma. The dream provides you with a deeper understanding and a clearer awareness of your soul's evolvement. The imagery and content of the dream shows the spiritual aspect of your physical reality.

DECIPHERING YOUR DREAMS

Many of your dreams are consciously forgotten or misunderstood only because you believe your dreams are difficult to remember and understand. Your belief becomes a self-fulfilling prophecy. If you want to remember and understand your dreams, then work with the same three qualities of desire, expectation, and belief that opened up your past-life memories. When you put your belief into action, your dreams will show themselves.

Deciphering dreams is easy, once you apply a few basic principles of the process of dreaming. Many people view their dreams as separate from themselves, and this causes them to misunderstand and misinterpret their dreams. As you dream, you're involved in the action; when you interpret your dreams, you tend to view yourself and the content of the dream as an outside observer, rather than an intimate participant. The events, imagery, and emotions in your dreams originate from your own thoughts, feelings, and experiences. When you understand how you perceive the information offered in your dreams, you can accurately interpret your dreams.

Your subconscious communicates through imagery and symbolism, creating pictures that show actions and describe feelings. Your dream imagery contains symbols that are very important. Once you understand the symbol, the message of the dream opens up. Your dreams relate specifically to your experiences and to your level of awareness. Your dream imagery is based on your perceptions of what the pictures and symbols mean to you.

Dreams are experienced in pictures and then translated into words. When you interpret your dreams you translate the images into words that reveal the meaning of the dream. If you place your dreams in a conscious perspective and try to twist them into a limited interpretation, they become distorted beyond recognition. If you respond to your dream by placing it into a logical sequence of either past or present, or real and unreal, you tend to get lost in understanding your dreams. You'll find that most, if not all, of the imagery and information has been lost or misunderstood in the translation and the transition from Alpha to Beta.

The most important part about understanding your dreams is to respect the manner in which they show themselves, and to value them as a special source of knowledge. To understand your dreams, interpret them in the manner and spirit in which they're given. You dream in an Alpha level, so interpret your dream in an Alpha level. Dissecting your dreams in Beta will destroy their true meaning. Allowing Alpha to answer your questions about the dream will give you an accurate interpretation of your dream. The key to understanding your dreams is to recognize that your subconscious has the truth and is willing to share it with you.

Decipher your dreams by what your feelings are about the dream, and by determining the content and context of the dream. Note what you were doing in the dream and what happened in the dream. Note all the perceptions and feelings you have about the dream. Since your dream imagery originates in your subconscious, ask yourself how you feel about the events portrayed in your dream. See how the dream relates to your current experiences and emotions, and look for the past that could be reflected in present images.

Some of your past-life dreams may be easy to interpret, because the dreams are literal, and the images are clear. If your dreams are difficult to understand, they could be showing you emotions and events from your past lives that you're not yet ready to become aware of and accept, and you may need to further discover and explore the images that your dreams offer you. Your subconscious gives you images and symbols in your dreams that will help you understand an important message in your present life. Look deeper within the images to discover what your subconscious is saying to you.

There are specific items to look for in recognizing a past-life dream. Look for any similarities in present situations that could be reflections of past-life events. This will help you clarify whether the dream relates to your present life or your past lives. Note any images that directly relate to a past era of time, such as the architecture, the scenery, and the style of dress. Note any scenes or images that are out of sync with the main flow of the dream. These may represent things you've seen or done, or places you've been in your past lives, and your subconscious inserts them into your dream where they stick out like a sore thumb. Pay attention to your feelings about your dreams. A past-life dream can show itself in many different ways, and your feelings will help you discover the dreams that show you the pictures of your past lives.

PLANNING PAST-LIFE DREAMS

You can plan and program a past-life dream. Before you go to sleep, give yourself positive suggestions for dreaming about a past life. Your subconscious will select the past life that is most appropriate for you to become aware of. A general suggestion might be something like this:

As I sleep tonight, I'll dream about one of my past lives. I'll see the images very clearly, and I'll remember every detail about my dream. In the morning, I'll understand my dream perfectly. I'll interpret it accurately, and I'll understand all the past-life connections with my present life. I'll be able to use the knowledge I gain to help me in my present life.

This may sound like a lengthy suggestion, but it lays the groundwork for opening up, remembering, interpreting, understanding, and allowing your past-life dreams to help you. If you already have some information about one of your past lives, you can be more specific with your suggestion. As you're giving yourself the suggestions, you may become aware of an image or a feeling about a past life. This is your subconscious mind tuning into one of your past lives and giving you a preview of coming attractions.

Opening-Up Exercises

Plan and program past-life dreams. In your journal, write down all the dreams you have. Include your feelings about the dream and the symbols in your dream. Determine whether each dream is about one of your past lives or whether it relates only to your present life by looking at the overall message in your dream. Connect your past-life dreams to the events and experiences in your present life. Write down all the information and insights that your dreams offer you.

Because dreams are so valuable in every aspect of your life, begin a dream diary and write down all the dreams you have. This will help you understand their true meanings, and will help you get more in touch with your inner knowledge and your spiritual nature. Interpreting your dreams will improve your understanding and recognition of subconscious symbols and images, and will show you how your dreams communicate with you.

As you continue to record your dreams, they'll become clearer and more complete. They'll offer you insights into yourself, and answers to all the questions you have about your past lives. From time to time, review your notes about your dreams. You may find answers to questions you haven't asked yet, and answers to questions you weren't even aware of until you found the answer. Your dreams will reveal pictures of your past lives and will help you discover and understand everything you want to know.

11

Separate Selves and Spirituality

There's more to you than meets the eye. The world within yourself reveals many faces and facets of self-awareness, both past and present. As you begin to understand the outer expression of your experiences, and accept and acknowledge your thoughts and feelings about them, you develop your inner awareness and expand your knowledge. You become more aware of your feelings below the surface that rise up for your recognition, and you find that your feelings provide you with the understanding that enables you to become aware of the full extent of your experiences. As you continue on your journey of self-awareness and spiritual knowledge, you begin to realize that in discovering your past lives, you're discovering your "self" and your soul.

Your inner self is your feeling self, and contains all your emotions and experiences. Your higher self is your knowledgeable self, and has complete awareness and understanding of your inner truth and knowledge. Your higher self is the connecting link to your soul. Your soul is the essence of all that you are, and is within the accumulated awareness of your inner self and your higher self.

Your soul incorporates all the experiences and knowledge from your past lives into your present experiences and knowledge.

Your present incarnation is experienced and expressed through all aspects of your inner self and your higher self. Your feelings form the beginnings of your experiences. As you become in touch with your feelings, you recognize your inner self. Through your experiences, you acquire knowledge. Through this connection, you tune into the truth you have within yourself, and you become aware of your higher self. By understanding and applying your knowledge, you become aware of your soul.

Your self-awareness begins within you and is expressed through your emotions and experiences, through your inner knowledge and truth, and through the way you live your life and what you believe in. As you go within all the aspects of yourself, you completely understand your experiences and emotions, in both your present and your past lives, by viewing them with increased awareness. This puts you in touch with your truth. You gain the knowledge of how your past experiences relate to your present experiences, and you understand why your past-life memories surface to help you in your present life.

Your feelings, knowledge, and awareness compose the sum total of who you are from the inside out. By understanding your past lives from the awareness of your soul, and by filtering your awareness through the knowledge of your higher self and the feelings of your inner self, you affect and change your feelings and experiences, and you increase your knowledge as you acquire awareness. This awareness is then spiraled into your inner self and your higher self. It's a continuous cycle of growth and learning and evolvement.

YOUR INNER SELF

Your inner self is within you, and through your inner self you become aware of your true feelings about everything in your life. Your inner self translates your feelings into truth. This helps you understand your past-life emotions and experiences and their influence on your present life. Your inner self is your constant companion and confidant, and is the keeper of subconscious secrets. Your inner self knows the true reality of the world around you and the world within you.

You've been aware of your inner self all your life through your feelings. You're in touch with your inner self when you're quiet within yourself, to sort out your thoughts and experiences and to find out how you really feel about things. Your inner self helps you discover why you feel the way you do, and is your sounding board that reflects how you respond and react to everything in your life.

Your inner self knows your true feelings and brings them into a conscious level for you through your emotions and reactions to your experiences. Your inner self counsels you and gives you guidance through your feelings. No matter what the circumstances are, your inner self sees through all facades and clearly recognizes the truth. By following your feelings, you instinctively and intuitively know what is right for you.

All you have to do to know the truth about everything is to trust your feelings and believe in yourself. Trust begins within yourself. As you get in touch with yourself, you learn how to trust your feelings and responses to the events in your life, and this teaches you how to trust your inner self, and how to follow your feelings. As you trust yourself, you recognize the truth within. This helps you enormously in understanding your past-life memories, and in showing you all the facets of your experiences.

You may also be aware of your inner self as the little voice within that whispers to you from the quietness of your mind. Your inner voice is sometimes referred to as hunches, intuition, or a sense of just knowing something. Your inner self talks to you through your inner voice and your feelings, and speaks the truth at all times. When you trust yourself and you listen to the voice within, you'll always hear the truth. The more you listen to your inner voice, and the more you trust your inner self, the more you'll hear and be aware of.

Opening-Up Exercises

To really be in touch with your inner self and to listen to the voice within, you have to tune out distractions and conscious mind chatter. It's much easier to be in touch with your inner self in a natural, peaceful setting. You're more receptive to hearing and listening to your inner voice when you're in a quiet, relaxing place. You can find this place within your mind by placing your thoughts and feelings into a nature scene, where you're in tune with the quietness and gentleness of nature and with yourself. You can create an inner sanctuary, which is a special place within yourself, where you experience harmony with your inner self, and you feel the joy of just being who you are.

Your inner sanctuary is very peaceful and tranquil, where you can find solitude, and where you can allow yourself to be yourself. It's where you can look within yourself to quietly reflect on your feelings about the events that are happening in your life. It's where you can hear and listen to your inner voice and find answers to the questions you pose. It's where you can be in touch with your inner self and understand your feelings, and where you can trust yourself to know the truth.

Your sanctuary can be a beach, where you hear the sound of the waves and feel the warmth of the sun. It can be a forest, where you hear the sound of the wind gently moving the leaves in the trees. It can be an open field, where you see the horizon in all directions. It can be a mountain, with a clear and sparkling waterfall. It can be a garden, with very beautiful flowers.

Your inner sanctuary can be wherever and whatever you want it to be. It can be a place you've been before, or it can be a place you create within your mind. Your sanctuary may be symbolic of a feeling you've had, or a place you've been, where you really felt like yourself and enjoyed just being natural. It can represent a mood you've experienced where you truly felt in touch with yourself and in tune with nature.

Creating Your Inner Sanctuary

Imagine a natural, peaceful setting where you can be in touch with your inner self and in tune with nature. Enter an Alpha level and create your inner sanctuary in your mind. See and feel and be in your inner sanctuary. Enjoy feeling peaceful and quiet within yourself. Allow yourself to experience the quietness and gentleness of nature as you open up your awareness of your inner self.

In your journal, describe how you feel about yourself and what your thoughts are when you're being natural and in tune with yourself. This will help you become aware of how to get in touch with your feelings and how your inner truth and knowledge presents itself. Describe what your inner sanctuary looks like, and note the images you became aware of. The images may be symbolic of some of your deep, inner feelings. Interpret the images to discover why they've surfaced in your inner sanctuary. Get in touch with your feelings about them and what they represent to you.

Once you've created your inner sanctuary, you can go there whenever you want to and for any reason. You can go there to be in touch with your inner self and to know your true feelings. You can go there to listen to your inner voice and to hear the truth. In the quietness of your inner sanctuary, you can relax and feel peaceful. You can experience harmony within yourself and feel the joy of just "being." You can go within yourself to open up your past-life memories, and to see how they're reflected in your present emotions and experiences. As you become in touch with your feelings and listen to your thoughts, you gain insight and understanding into why you react the way you do in the present to your past-life emotions and experiences.

The Key to Knowledge
As you go within yourself, you experience harmony with nature and with yourself. You tune into your natural awareness of who you are by being in touch with your true feelings and by trusting yourself. As you do this, you open up your inner knowledge and you become aware that you already have the truth within. You become aware that you have the key to knowledge. As you go within yourself, your awareness and your inner truth open up more and more, enabling you to be in touch with your inner self, and allowing you to become in tune with your higher self.

In the following meditation, you'll explore the sunrise and experience the dawning of the light within you, as you discover your key to knowledge. The key opens up your understanding of yourself by unlocking the doorways to your inner feelings and truth, to your experiences and past-life memories, and to the essence of your soul. Before you begin, enter an Alpha level and be in touch with yourself in your inner sanctuary. Allow yourself to see, feel, and be in the images described in the meditation.

It's only moments before dawn. It's a beautiful summer morning and you're outside, enjoying the beginning of a new day. You're aware of a gentle, warm breeze and the scent of the morning air. You can hear birds chirping in the distance, and the sound is muted and pleasant as they welcome the dawn of a new day.

You see a very peaceful place to relax in front of you. There are a few trees, and the ground is covered with grass. You begin to walk toward it, thinking that maybe you'd like to relax there while you enjoy the sunrise. The grass feels like velvet beneath your feet, and as you walk, you feel freer than you've ever felt before.

There's a beach nearby. You can hear the sound of the waves and you think you'd enjoy the sunrise even more if you were at the beach. You begin to walk toward the beach, and as the beach comes into view, you can see the waves as they gently touch the shore.

As you look at the sky, you notice that it's getting lighter and lighter. You have a clear view of the horizon as the water seemingly touches the sky at a distance. You can see the first rays of the sunrise begin to come over the horizon, and the colors are reflected and mirrored on the water.

You can see a few clouds in the morning sky, and you notice that the clouds are tinged with the early colors of dawn. Pale orange at first, and then the pale orange blends into a shade of pink that you've never really seen before. It's almost as if pearls are coloring the bottom of the clouds, or maybe the water is reflecting the color of the sunrise onto the clouds.

You realize that you're seeing the colors of dawn for the first time in a very special way. The beauty and clarity of the colors inspire a sense of awe and wonderment inside of you as you realize you're seeing the colors of a new day . . . the colors of a new beginning. As you close your eyes and sense the colors, the colors become more beautiful inside you. You can feel the colors of dawn, and you hear the magical melody they play within your mind.

And now you realize that you are the colors of dawn. You are the colors of the sunrise. In essence, you have become the sunrise. The colors seem to rise to make room for the golden color of the sun. The sun is above the horizon now, and you're rising with the sun. As the sun continues to rise higher and higher in the sky, you continue to rise with it. The feeling is exhilarating and you feel more alive than you've ever felt before.

And now you're going beyond the sunrise . . . beyond the colors of dawn into the center of the sunrise. You've entered a special and magical place within yourself, and it feels like you've always been there. You've always known the way to this most special and magical place.

As you look to your right, you'll see a golden key that has been formed by the sunrise, and by the colors of dawn. This golden key opens your inner knowledge and truth. Reach for the golden key. Hold it within your hand, and feel its warmth. Feel it pulsate with positive energy and power. Hold the key within your heart, and feel yourself becoming aware of your inner truth. Hold the key within your mind, and understand its treasures. Feel your mind opening up and expanding into knowledge and awareness. Hold the key within your soul and feel yourself becoming aware of the light within you.

*　*　*　*　*

The golden key you hold within your hand, and within your heart, and mind, and soul, belongs to you. You've explored a very special part of yourself and you've found a treasure more valuable and precious than any other treasure the world has to offer. You've found a golden key that opens all the positive and powerful treasures of your mind and your soul.

You see a golden sun ray that radiates from the sunrise. You notice how the sun ray originates from the sun, and how it travels from its source to gently touch the earth to light the way of a beautiful new day. You notice that it shines on the beach where you watched the dawn begin. Become part of that golden sun ray and travel with it into your very special and peaceful place on the beach where you enjoyed the beginning of the sunrise.

And now you're standing on the beach again, and you notice that the sun is completely above the horizon. Look at the golden key you hold in your hand, and look at the sunrise again. The colors are different now. They've all blended into a golden color . . . the color of the key . . . the color of the sun . . . and the color of knowledge. You can feel the color within your mind, and the golden color feels more beautiful than ever before.

The sky is a very bright blue, and the clouds that reflected the colors of the sunrise now reflect the color of gold. And even as you look at the clouds that are golden, they change to a pure white . . . as if they've absorbed the golden sunrise . . . as if they're holding and keeping safe the colors of dawn for the next sunrise.

You're aware of the warmth of the sun. You're aware of a gentle breeze and the scent of the morning air. You're aware of the sound of birds, chirping in the distance. You can hear the melody they sing as they welcome the sunshine. And you're aware of the golden key you hold within your mind. You're aware that you hold the key to knowledge.

The sun is a universal symbol of awareness and knowledge and light. In this meditation, the sunrise represented the opening up and expanding of your inner truth and knowledge. In your journal, write down everything you experienced in your meditation. Note all your feelings and thoughts as you felt yourself opening up your inner knowledge, and as you became aware of the truth within you. Write down all the images you became aware of as you increased your level of awareness by going within the center of the sunrise, and within the center of your soul.

YOUR HIGHER SELF

Your higher self is the more wise and knowing part of you, and is aware of everything about you. Your higher self offers you direction and guidance in your life on both a physical and a spiritual level. As you become aware of your higher self, and you open up your inner knowledge and truth, you enable yourself to live on a more aware level. By experiencing all the aspects of your life in and through and from the perspective of your higher self, you increase your knowledge and awareness.

Your higher self is within all the aspects of your life, from the mundane to the magical. You can give all your everyday problems, cares, and worries to your higher self, and your higher self will handle them with understanding and knowledge, and will show you how to take care of them. You can go to your higher self for any reason, and your higher self will understand and accept whatever you're feeling and experiencing and will show you how to understand yourself in a better and clearer way.

Your higher self is your teacher and your mentor. Through all your experiences, both past and present, you gain understanding into yourself. You acquire knowledge from your experiences, and through your knowledge you become aware of your truth. By knowing your truth, you advance to higher levels of learning.

Your higher self is your guide and will lead you, with understanding and insight, into and through your past-life memories. You can go through your higher self to achieve full awareness of all the events and emotions you experienced in your past lives. Your higher self can help you become aware of your present responses to past-life events by explaining how the experience relates to your present life. You can ask your higher self for answers about a problem that has its origins in a past life. Your higher self will show you how to connect with the past-life experience in order to understand and resolve the problem.

Your higher self can explain who the people in your present life were in past lives, and what your relationship with them was in the past. Your higher self will show you the karma that was incurred between you, and will explain the reasons for being together with them again. Your higher self will help you understand all aspects of your karma, and will guide you through the balancing process.

Your higher self opens the communication between your physical existence and experiences and your spiritual understanding of yourself and your awareness. Your higher self is the liaison between your feelings and your spirituality, and serves as the intermediary between the expression of your physical experiences and the expression of your spiritual awareness.

Your higher self is a universal channel of knowledge, awareness, and light, and is the link to your spirituality. Your higher self will show you the world of knowledge, and will help you step up into the spiritual realms of awareness, as you reach for enlightenment within yourself. Through the wisdom and knowledge of your higher self, you become aware of your soul and you understand your true spiritual nature.

Opening-Up Exercise

You can perceive your higher self in many different ways. Everyone becomes aware of their higher self in a way that is unique to them. Some people sense their higher self as an energy or a feeling; others see their higher self as an image of themselves that is knowledgeable and wise in every respect. Some higher selves appear symbolically as wise old men, ancient philosophers, or teachers; some show themselves as a mother or father figure, who is nurturing, caring, and comforting. Your higher self is a culmination of all the knowledge you've acquired and all the experiences you've had in every lifetime. As you become aware of your higher self, you become aware of yourself.

Your higher self is a very, very special part of you. You've known your higher self forever, in every lifetime you've ever experienced, and in all the time you've spent together in the interim between lives. There's a bond between you that has been formed since the beginning of time, and forged throughout your soul's entire existence. Reuniting with your higher self is like being with your oldest, dearest, and most trusted friend. It's the most natural thing in the world; it feels like coming home after a long journey where you were lost, hungry, afraid, and alone. If you've been out of touch with your higher self, the reunion is sometimes emotional, filled with a joy and happiness that words cannot describe.

Reuniting With Your Higher Self

In the following meditation, allow yourself to become aware of your higher self, and to reestablish the bond between you. Before you begin, enter an Alpha level and go into your inner sanctuary. Feel peaceful and quiet within yourself.

In your inner sanctuary, you feel in touch with yourself and in tune with nature. You feel very peaceful and quiet, and you feel a special sense of awareness building inside of you. As you look around your sanctuary, you'll see your higher self waiting for you. As you look at your higher self, you experience an incredible feeling of respect and trust.

As your higher self begins to walk toward you, you feel very positive feelings that emanate from your higher self, and you sense the energy and knowledge that radiate from within your higher self. As you move forward to reunite with your higher self, you experience a wonderful feeling of joy and happiness. As your higher self embraces you, you feel yourself merging into knowledge and awareness and light. You know you've found what you've been looking for. You've found the higher aspect of yourself.

In your own way, and in the manner that feels most right for you, become more in tune with your higher self. Begin to build a rapport with your higher self that strengthens the bond between you as you open up your inner knowledge and awareness. When you're done with your meditation, just breathe deeply for a few moments, feeling the harmony within yourself and with your higher self. Breathe in the awareness and the understanding of everything you've discovered about your higher self.

In your journal, write down everything you experienced and became aware of as you reunited with your higher self. Write down all your feelings and thoughts about your higher self. Note what your higher self said to you, and how your higher self appeared to you. Note what your higher self did, and how you responded to your higher self. Define and describe your higher self. This will help you become even more aware of your higher self and all the knowledge you have within you. Knowing your higher self is a prelude to becoming aware of your soul and understanding your spiritual nature.

THE ESSENCE OF YOUR SOUL

A soul is the intangible and viable life source and spirit within you, which is immortal. Your soul is the essence of all that you are, and is the energy and awareness that comprises you. Your soul is the totality of all your experiences, and your cumulative thoughts, feelings, and knowledge. Your past lives, and all the events and emotions contained within them, are an integral and inseparable part of you.

As you become in touch with your inner self and your feelings, and you become in tune with your higher self and your knowledge, you also become aware of your soul and the truth within yourself. Trying to define a soul in a way that will fit everyone's perception of a soul is like trying to catch an elusive butterfly. Words fall short of an accurate interpretation and a clear description of what a soul is.

A very enlightening definition of a soul was overheard at a funeral. After their uncle's death, two little philosophers, ages five and six, were discussing where his soul was. Both agreed that he was happy and his soul was in heaven, because he was a nice person. Following this agreement, they began a discussion of what a soul is. One child said that a soul is a person's mind and their thoughts. The other one said that a soul is what's inside a person's heart and their feelings.

After they defined what a soul is, and agreed that they were both right, they began another discussion of where heaven was, and what it was like. They decided that heaven was a misty place beyond the clouds, and it was probably a comfortable place to go to sleep for awhile and to dream, before your soul woke up again and had to go to work in heaven.

Feeling satisfied that heaven was a nice place to be, they began a friendly argument about what a soul looks like. One child said a soul would look like a star if you were in heaven. If you weren't in heaven, your soul would look like a ghost. The other one stated, with absolute conviction, that a soul looked just like lights that moved, and you could see it and touch it. At this point, their mother stepped into the discussion and suggested that if they looked into their own eyes, they'd be able to see their souls. This settled the argument and they began a staring contest.

Opening-Up Exercises

Exercise 1. You can best define your own soul by your feelings and thoughts about it, and by what you believe it to be. In your journal, write down your answers to the following questions. Give your answers careful thought and really get in touch with your feelings about your soul.

- Define and describe, in general terms, what a soul is. Your idea of what a soul is will provide you with a frame of reference to get you on course for the next several questions.
- Define and describe, in specific terms, what *your* soul is. What, exactly, is your soul, and what is it really like? How do you perceive it? What essence or life source is your soul composed of? How does it manifest and express itself in your present life? Your answers will help you get in touch with your awareness of your soul, and your beliefs about spirituality and immortality.
- Describe what your soul looks like, and draw a picture of it. Interpret your picture to discover what the images show. The images are usually symbolic and represent your spiritual interpretation of your soul.

Exercise 2. The following meditations will help you discover more about your soul. Volumes have been written on what a soul is, and on what spirituality is all about. Although books can provide you with an understanding about the subject, they reflect someone else's interpretation of what they perceive a soul to be, based on their experiences and frame of reference.

Discover the truth for yourself, and understand your own unique experiences. In this way, you'll understand your soul and you'll know what your spirituality is all about. As you become aware of your soul, you receive an understanding of yourself that no amount of words can give you. As you experience the awareness of your soul, you discover the essence of yourself. You find out who you really are, from the inside out.

Seeing Your Soul

As you look within yourself, you see the intangible aspects of your soul, and you understand how you perceive your soul. Begin your meditation by entering an Alpha level and going into your inner sanctuary. Feel quiet and peaceful within yourself, as you become in tune with nature and in harmony with your higher self. Allow your higher self to guide you as you see your soul in the way that is most appropriate for you. Be receptive to seeing the images, hearing the thoughts, and sensing the feelings that your higher self provides.

Look within yourself to see the inner qualities of your soul as they're reflected in your thoughts and beliefs, and expressed through your emotions and experiences. At first, you may become aware of your inner feelings and your ideas, dreams, and goals. You may find some revealing insights into how you really feel about yourself. You may become in touch with your true feelings about who you are now, and what you want to accomplish in this lifetime. You may discover some valuable clues to your purpose and destiny.

As you look even more deeply within yourself, and get more in touch with your inner truth and knowledge, you open up your awareness of your soul. You may begin to see images of both your present and your past lives that show you the qualities of your soul and how they're expressed. In a powerful and positive way, you'll begin to tune into the energy vibrations of your soul, as you become aware of the nature of your spirituality.

In your journal, write down everything you became aware of in your meditation. Note all the images, thoughts, and feelings that represent the intangible qualities of your soul, and the various aspects of yourself and your experiences. Write down how you perceived your soul, and how your spirituality is expressed through your thoughts, feelings, and experiences.

Faces From the Past

Your eyes are the window to the world within you and the mirror of your soul. After you become aware of the intangible qualities of your soul (through the first meditation) and how you express them in your present life, you can begin to see the more tangible vision of your soul as you appeared in your past lives. Your soul is mirrored in your eyes, and you can see the reflection of who you were in your past lives by looking at and through your eyes in a mirror to see the many faces of your soul.

(Note: This meditation is very serious. If you're not prepared for what you may experience by first being in tune with your higher self, then wait until you feel you're ready. If you proceed without being in an Alpha level and without being guided by your higher self, you'll experience one of two things. You'll either become frightened by what you see, because you won't be able to understand it, or you'll just see yourself looking at your reflection, and wishing you'd achieved the proper level of mind first.)

Before you begin, enter an Alpha level and raise your awareness to be in tune with your higher self. As you do this, you'll feel your mind becoming more and more aware as you open up your inner truth and knowledge. After you've achieved a more aware level of mind, open your eyes and begin the meditation. Allow your higher self to guide you and give you answers and understanding into everything you experience.

Look at yourself, as you are now, in a mirror. You'll see a physical reflection of your soul in this lifetime. Concentrate on your eyes, and pay attention to your thoughts and feelings. Begin to move past your physical appearance into the realms of spiritual awareness, where you're able to see the individual images of your soul as you appeared in previous incarnations. You may begin to see facial features that become superimposed on your mirror image, or you may sense your faces from the past without physically seeing them.

As you see your faces from the past, you receive an understanding and awareness into those previous lifetimes and the influence they have on your present life. As you meditate on the images you see, you become aware of who you were before and how the experiences in your past lives have shaped and molded your awareness into who you are now. You're able to see how your soul has progressed in its evolvement.

In your journal, write down everything you experienced and became aware of in your meditation. Note all the images you saw of yourself, and your thoughts and feelings about each image. Note all the insights and information you became aware of regarding who you were, and what you did in your past lives. Note all the connections to your present life. Write down your understanding of the experiences from your past lives that show you how your soul has progressed from the past into the present. (More information is presented on inner self, higher self, and soul in Chapter 19.)

12

Visiting the Visions
of Your Past Lives

As you remember and reexperience your past lives, keep in mind that your memories aren't affected by time. Your past lives are just as real in the present as they were in the past. The energies that surround past-life events and emotions survive in the present. When you're remembering the past in the present, you're reexperiencing the past *as* the present. The two are so interwoven that they become just like one. Your past life may have occurred five hundred years ago, but the way you respond to the events and emotions from the past is just as clear and real as if your past life occurred five minutes ago.

This is due to the flow of energy that filters through time because of the influence the past life has on your present life. When you remember and reexperience a past-life memory, you blend the energies of past and present together. Through your awareness of your past life, and your understanding of how it affects your present life, the energy is shared between the past and the present. Because you're viewing the memory from the present, the past is experienced in a current framework of time.

Your past-life trips offer you an interesting and enlightening journey of self-discovery. You'll be in your past lives while you remain connected with your present life. Your method of travel will be mind projection. Your guide will be your higher self. The ticket to your past-life trips offers you the opportunity to learn more about yourself by discovering what you did, and what happened to you in your past lives. You can explore who you were before, and you can reexperience past-life events. You can see how your past influences and affects your present. The souvenirs and treasures of your trips will be acquiring insights and knowledge from your past lives, and understanding how and why the past connects with the present.

There are several ways to view and experience the events and emotions from your past lives. You can visit the visions of your past lives without feeling the emotions, or you can experience them by reliving the events and emotions—or you can do both at the same time. You can see, feel, and be in and out of your past lives, simultaneously or separately, by experiencing them from different perspectives. Some perspectives will place you directly in your past life; others will give you a bird's-eye view. As you explore your past lives, you'll experience different views and vantage points of your memories that will offer you the most understanding and awareness of a past life.

Experiential: This perspective will place your awareness directly into your past-life memory, and will allow you to experience it, with all of the attendant emotions and events that are attached to the memory. You'll see, hear, feel, smell, and taste the images from the past. Your awareness will be absorbed in the scene and completely encompassed within everything you're experiencing. When your awareness is immersed in your past life, you're feeling the emotions, and you're experiencing the events. This helps you understand the feelings you may have carried forward to this lifetime that are influencing and affecting you in present situations.

Detachment: This perspective will remove you emotionally from your memory while you remain involved in the scene. You'll experience the past-life event without feeling the emotions. It will feel as if the event were happening to someone else, and you'll obtain all the benefits of fully experiencing the event and the emotions, but you won't feel them. This is especially beneficial if the memory is painful or traumatic, because it gives you the objectivity to experience the emotions of the event in a clear way.

Overview: This perspective will place your awareness above the past-life event as you participate in it. You'll be aware of all the aspects of the event, and your understanding of what you experience in the event will be expanded. You're sharing your awareness between viewing the event and completely understanding it, and being in the event and experiencing it. This offers you the option of placing more of your awareness into either seeing the event or experiencing the event. Your choice will be determined by what you want to do, and by what the event is.

When you place your awareness within the event, you're actively participating in the scene and feeling everything about the event. When you place your awareness above the scene, you understand the reasons why the event occurred, and why you acted the way you did. You gain insights and answers from the perspective of your higher self. This helps you understand the origins of the event and the purpose of your previous actions. You can incorporate both the experiential and detachment perspectives within the overview method. This is like a seesaw effect, and both vantage points are part and parcel of each other.

You can visit and view the visions from your past lives through one or all of the perspectives. You may find yourself in one perspective that flows into a different perspective that offers you more insight and information about your past life. You'll be visiting the visions of your past lives in the way that is most appropriate for you to experience them.

PREPARING FOR YOUR TRIPS INTO THE PAST
Before you go on your mind trips to visit the visions from your past, there are a few things to be aware of and to prepare for. The

past lives you reexperience will be the ones that are important to your present life. As you reexperience the past, you'll be able to see the connections between the past and the present. Allow yourself to travel without excess baggage. Let go of conscious restrictions that will interfere with your journeys into your past lives. Take with you an increased awareness of all the events and emotions you'll be experiencing; allow yourself to understand everything you encounter. Bring the souvenirs of understanding and knowledge with you when you return to the present.

During your trips, you may experience some physical responses, such as rapid eye movement. This occurs because you're using your mind's eye to see the scenes. You may find that you have to swallow a lot. This is due to feeling deeply relaxed. Your body may feel very expansive or very light, or it may feel like it's vibrating with energy. You may also experience a feeling of floating above your body. This is due to the increased energy of the white light (which is a spiritual protection that will be explained shortly) and to your increased level of awareness.

As you begin to travel into the past, you may feel like you're moving through a tunnel with muted lights that dart back and forth, and pleasant sounds that rush or swish by you. This can occur as you enter higher levels of spiritual awareness, and you synchronize your energy with these levels. You may become aware of a buzzing sensation around your body and in your ears. This occurs because you're traveling through time and energy.

As you return to the present, you may feel yourself moving through what seems to be layers of energy, and as you enter the present they feel heavier. This is because physical energy is slower than spiritual energy. All of these responses are normal and natural; you may experience some of them, none of them, or all of them in varying degrees, depending on your frame of mind and level of awareness, and your involvement with your trip.

In your past lives, you'll find some happy and pleasant memories, and you'll probably find some that aren't so pleasant. There could be a few terrible things lurking in the shadows from the past just waiting to haunt you. You may have done things or experienced events that were painful and traumatic, and the emotions from those events may still affect you.

For any number of reasons, it can be beneficial to reexperience the memory, and to feel your emotions from the past. Sometimes, the only way to be free of negative past-life influences is to acknowledge and accept them. Once you understand them, you can let them go. By reliving the deep and dark emotions, you understand both your past and present reactions to the past-life experience. You discover how you're responding to the past-life memory now, and you obtain very revealing answers into present situations that are influenced by past-life events. You get to the cause and understand the origin of past-life events that affect your present life. This increases your understanding of past/present connections by showing you how the past is reflected in the present. In reexperiencing painful or traumatic events from your past lives, follow your own judgment and intuitive knowledge.

The awareness of your past-life memories is filtered through your level of understanding and receptivity. If you're not ready or prepared to remember a particular past-life event, your subconscious has a built-in safety valve that will prevent you from remembering that particular aspect of your past life. The event you're experiencing will go absolutely blank, devoid of images and empty of feelings. You may also find your awareness catapulted into the present. This creates a rapid change in energies, which you may experience as your body suddenly shaking or jerking in a sharp movement.

Remembering the events and emotions from your past lives is very serious. If you feel apprehensive about mind-projecting into your memories, then wait until you feel you're ready. Your trips are an in-depth meditation and a do-it-yourself past-life regression that your higher self will guide you into and through. As you approach and engage in your trips, it is imperative that you follow the direction of your higher self.

When you remember and reexperience past-life events, you may bring some of those past feelings into your present life. The energies that surround events you participated in still exist, and this energy can be brought into the present if you're not protected. Any negative feelings, energies, and influences from a past life belong in the past, not the present.

If you feel any bad vibes during or after your trips into the past, it's important to let go of these negative feelings and leave them in the past. A white-light protection will shield you during your trips and will keep you from being affected by and from bringing any negative energies into the present. The positive energies you bring into the present are the awareness and understanding of what occurred in your past lives, so you can use the knowledge to help you in your present life.

WHITE-LIGHT PROTECTION

You can protect yourself with the pure and positive energies of white light. The white-light protection is a universal energy and a powerful source you can draw from at any time you may need it and for any reason. By surrounding yourself with a white-light protection, you keep yourself safe on a physical, emotional, mental, and spiritual level from feeling any negative past-life energies, and from bringing them into your present life. It keeps the energies and your awareness of past-life events and emotions on a positive level. You can remember and reexperience everything in your past lives and learn from them without being affected by any negativity.

Enter an Alpha level and go through the rainbow into the white mist above the rainbow. The mist is a universal white light that is very powerful, and very pure and positive in its energy vibration. See and sense and feel yourself in the mist above the rainbow. It feels peaceful, comforting, and warm. Immerse yourself in it completely.

Breathe it inside of you. It feels like a breath of pure, fresh air that revitalizes and replenishes your energy on every level of your body, your mind, and your soul. Feel the warmth that flows through your body like a heartbeat, pulsating in a rhythm of protection and safety that feels natural and comfortable as it rejuvenates you with pure and positive energy.

Feel the energy inside of you as it surrounds every muscle, every bone, every tissue, and every organ in your physical body. As the warmth begins to flow through you, you may feel yourself vibrating with the pure and positive energy. As the white light enters your mind, and you accept it and absorb it within yourself, you feel your level of awareness expanding.

Feel the vibrations of energy as you surround your body with the white light of physical, emotional, mental, and spiritual protection. Wrap the light around you like a warm and safe cloak of awareness and knowledge and energy. Feel it surrounding you with positive energy and protection. It's a universal source of energy that blends with your energy, both within you and around you, and keeps you safe on all levels. Feel your increased energy and your expanded awareness as you completely encircle yourself with the white light.

You have access to the white light any time you may need it, just by thinking about it. The white light will cleanse and purify your energies and will shield you from any and all negative energy vibrations and feelings you may encounter. It is of utmost importance that you protect yourself from past-life pain or trauma. By completely encircling yourself with white light, both inside and outside your physical body and your mind, you're protected from reexperiencing any negative energy vibrations and from bringing their influence into your present life.

(Note: If you're not protected with the white light, you can bring past-life energies into the present where they may adversely affect you. This is similar to when you have a bad experience in your present life. The energies cling to you for awhile, before they gradually wear off. The negative energy from past-life events causes a temporary shock to your system, due to the difference in energies and to your present reactions to past-life events. The past can seem very real in the present. Past-life emotions and your present reactions to them can be a bit overwhelming if they're not placed in their proper perspective and time frame, and understood in their appropriate context. If this occurs, you can rid yourself of any negativity by completely immersing yourself in the white light. This will cleanse and purify the past-life energies, and return you to your present energies.)

GROUNDING AND CENTERING

Grounding yourself allows you to remain aware of your physical body and your surroundings in the present time as you reexperience events and emotions from your past lives. Grounding firmly connects you with physical energies as you enter spiritual energies. The importance of being connected with your present surroundings is vital. It keeps you physically oriented in the present, while it allows you to immerse yourself in your higher spiritual energies.

Ground yourself by touching and being aware of a physical object. If you're sitting in a chair, place your feet firmly on the floor, and place your hands by your sides so you're touching the fabric and texture of the chair. If you're lying down, place your hands so they're in physical contact with something other than your body. You're secure in the present while you're free to explore the past.

Centering yourself allows you to be in both the past and present time, as you explore and experience events from your past lives. The benefits of sharing your awareness between your past and your present is invaluable in discovering details and understanding all the aspects of your memories and how they relate to your present life. This enables you to be aware of the past and the present simultaneously, and in synchronicity with each other.

Center yourself by entering an Alpha level and placing your awareness within yourself and within your past-life memories. Be equally aware of who you are now and who you were before. This keeps you aware of your present feelings as you become aware of your past-life emotions, and helps you understand all the connections between the two.

(Note: It's absolutely impossible to get lost in a past-life memory. The worst thing you can experience if you're not grounded and centered is a brief and temporary disorientation, just like waking up from sleep too fast.)

PROJECTING YOURSELF INTO YOUR PAST LIVES

Mind projection is something you've accomplished many times before. Whenever you daydream, have a reverie, or use your imagination, you've used mind projection. As you become totally involved with your thoughts and feelings, you experience the content of the daydream or reverie to the point where you feel you're actually in the scene, rather than being outside it and looking in from an observer's standpoint.

You've mind-projected when you've read a book or watched a movie and become so absorbed in the subject matter that you lost track of time and physical reality. It seemed as though the book or the movie was the reality. This is because you projected your awareness into the scene so completely that you experienced the scene.

Your subconscious already has the movie scripts of your past lives. All you have to do is run the projector. You can watch your past lives play out right in front of you in your mind's eye, and you can project yourself into the scenes. You can produce, direct, and star in your own past lives. You can freeze any frame of the movie to view the scenes in detail. You can move the images forward or backward, or stop them for a moment in time. You can either view the movie, or you can project yourself into the movie.

Lights, Camera, Action!!

The following visualization will help you project yourself into images and feelings, and will help you become more involved in your memories. Hopefully, you enjoy warm, sunny days at the beach. Draw upon your previous memories of when you were at a beach to become more involved in the scene. In addition to seeing the images, feel and sense and be in the images. Fill in the scene with your own memories, and change the scene to reflect your experiences. Enter an Alpha level and project your feelings and thoughts completely into the scene, so that you're totally experiencing it.

Remember a warm, sunny day when you were at the beach. You can hear the splash of the waves and the sound of the water as it comes to the shore. As you walk along the beach, you can feel the softness of the sand beneath your feet. You notice a few seashells that have been washed ashore by the tide, and you pick them up to admire them.

As you continue walking along the beach, you find a small, secluded cove next to some large rocks that stretch across the sand. It's quiet and private, and it's a perfect place to lie on your beach towel. As you get comfortable on your towel, you can feel the sand adjust to your body. As you lie on the beach, you begin to feel the warmth of the sun.

The sky is a perfect blue, with puffy white clouds. The sun is bright and strong, and feels pleasantly warm on your body. You can feel a gentle breeze, and you can smell the scent of your suntan lotion. You can hear the sound of seagulls, and the talk and laughter of other people in the distance. You feel so relaxed and peaceful, and the quiet hum of conversation sounds like soft and gentle music.

As you lie on the beach, you can hear the water as it comes to the shore, and as it returns to the ocean. As the tide ebbs and flows, your breathing begins to match the rhythm of the tide . . . in and out . . . back and forth. The sound of the ocean is lulling and soothing and relaxing. The sounds ebb and flow, and form a gentle, rhythmic pattern that moves in tune with your thoughts and your feelings.

The sun feels pleasantly warm on your body, and the sound of the ocean relaxes you more and more. All your thoughts flow into a perfect awareness of the beautiful day you're experiencing. You feel a wonderful sense of contentment and peace. You're enjoying the warmth of the sun and you're in harmony with everything you're experiencing.

When you project your awareness into a scene and become completely absorbed in the images, your conscious mind doesn't interfere with or intrude upon your thoughts and feelings. You may have felt as if you were lying on a sandy beach on a beautiful summer day, instead of reading this book. You may have actually felt the warmth of the sun on your body. You might even have gotten sunburned if you completely projected your awareness into the images, and became totally involved in the scene you were experiencing. As you engaged yourself in the sights, sounds, and feelings in the visualization, your subconscious brought forth memories of when you were at a beach, and recreated the scene so perfectly that you may have responded physically to the memory.

When you remember events from your past lives, you may become so involved in the memory that it seems as if it's more than a memory. This occurs when you completely project your thoughts and feelings into your past life. You reexperience the event in so much detail, and with such feeling, that the memory engages your full attention. This is very beneficial in exploring and experiencing the events and emotions that occurred in your past lives, because it gives you an increased awareness and understanding of those events and emotions.

MIND-TRIPPING INTO YOUR MEMORIES

When you project yourself into a past-life memory, your past life becomes an experience that you see and feel on a very real level. Mind-tripping into your memories is accomplished by projecting your thoughts and feelings into another place, in another time, and reexperiencing the events you've experienced before. When you're mind-tripping, you're involved in a do-it-yourself past-life regression. You can travel into your past lives as an observer or a participant. As an observer, you're outside the memory, and you watch your past life. As a participant, you're inside the memory, and you reexperience your past life.

You can visit the visions of your past lives by focusing your thoughts and feelings into certain areas of your memories to become aware of and to participate in events you've experienced before. Your thoughts and feelings travel as you enter the past, while they remain connected with you in the present. You experience your awareness in the past and the present at the same time. In mind projection, time doesn't exist. You can travel into the past, go into the future, or stay in the present. You can project yourself anywhere you want to go. You can travel to different places in time as easily as thinking about them. You're traveling on your thought energy, so all you have to do is think a thought and you're there.

Before you begin your trips, enter an Alpha level, surround yourself with the white-light protection, and center and ground yourself. As you embark on your journey, allow your higher self to guide you as you travel through your trips.

Opening-Up Exercises

Within your subconscious mind are all the memories of your past lives. You don't need a map to find them, and you don't need directions to discover where you've lived before. Your higher self already knows all about the memories and how to find them, and will show you the course to take to rediscover them. In your mind trip, you're free to explore the realms and realities of your past lives.

As you project your awareness into your past lives, you'll see and feel past-life events that have a direct influence on your present life. As you travel on the energy of your thoughts, allow your higher self to guide you, and to explain everything you want to know about your past lives. This will help you understand all the things you see and feel, and will give you insights and answers into everything you experience.

Tripping Through Time

You might want to practice mind-tripping, staying close to the present by exploring and experiencing a recent memory. This will help you get the "feel" of a mind trip. As you allow your awareness to travel outside of the immediate present, and you project yourself into the memory, notice the feelings and sensations you experience, and the thoughts and images you become aware of. One of the interesting things that occurs in a mind trip is that you become aware of details that escaped your attention the first time.

On your practice trip, enter an Alpha level and project your thoughts to a place you've been before in this life. Remember a pleasant and happy time you experienced there very recently. Project your awareness completely into seeing and feeling the previous event. Become aware of all your earlier thoughts and feelings. Become totally involved as you see and sense and feel the images of your memory. If you feel more comfortable viewing the scenes instead of projecting yourself into the scenes, then just imagine you're watching a movie and observe the action. Set your own pace and follow your own direction.

When you're done with your practice trip, begin to slowly focus on the present. Gradually bring your awareness into your present surroundings in the present time, remembering all of the sights, sounds, and scenes you experienced in your mind trip. Allow yourself a few moments to completely absorb all the information you became aware of, and to fully orient yourself into the present. (By moving slowly from the past through the transition of time into the present, you retain more information on a conscious level and you understand it better.)

In your journal, write down everything you experienced during your practice trip. Note all the information and images you became aware of. Note your thoughts and feelings before, during, and after your trip, and how you physically responded to the memory as you projected yourself into the previous event.

Countries, Cultures, and Civilizations
On your mind trip, you'll be projecting yourself into one of your past lives, and exploring and experiencing it either as an observer or a participant. As a reference point, choose a country, culture, or civilization where you feel you've lived before; or choose a place you feel drawn to that you'd like to visit to see if you've had a previous incarnation there. When you have a place in mind, choose an image or a symbol that, for you, represents the country, culture, or civilization you want to visit. Some examples are: Egypt/

pyramid; Atlantis/crystal; England/Stonehenge. Choose a symbol that you feel is most appropriate.

Center your awareness on the image that represents the place you want to visit. This will be the beginning of your mind trip as you project yourself into a specific place and point in time in one of your past lives. The image you choose will take you into an important event you experienced in your past life that affects you now, and will direct you to where you've lived before.

Once you've arrived, allow yourself to see and feel other images that relate to your past life in that country, culture, or civilization. At first, you may become aware of the landscape or scenery, or you may find yourself in the middle of an event that occurred in one of your past lives. Take a few moments to become familiar with the scene, and to acquaint yourself with what's happening. To begin with, you might want to share your awareness with both your feelings and your thoughts. Be equally aware of both at the same time, and notice how you feel and what your thoughts are.

Watch your past life play out as you watch yourself participate in your past life. This gives you a framework to further explore everything that is important to you. This also helps you decide whether you want to watch the scene or be in the scene. If you want to become more involved in your past life, project your thoughts and feelings into the images. Respect your feelings as to how far you want to project yourself into the memory.

Begin your trip by centering and grounding yourself. Enter an Alpha level, and breathe in the white-light protection. Focus on the image that represents a country where you've lived before. Allow your higher self to guide you as you project yourself into the image. As you do this, you may feel yourself being drawn to a particular culture or civilization that existed there before. As you become aware of a period of time and a place in time where you've lived before and you see the scene, completely project your thoughts and feelings into the country, culture, or civilization.

See yourself as you were before. See how you're dressed and what you're doing. Be aware of any sights or sounds that are around you. Be very aware of your thoughts and feelings. Discover things you've known before, and things you've done before. Discover who you were before. Explore and experience all the events and emotions in your past life. Allow yourself to completely understand everything you experience and become aware of about your past life.

When you're done with your mind trip, bring your awareness into the present time by focusing and directing your thoughts and feelings into who you are right now. As you orient yourself into the present, bring with you the awareness of everything you've experienced, and all the knowledge you've acquired about your past life that provides you with insight and understanding into your present life.

In your journal, write down everything you experienced and became aware of on your mind trip. Note all your thoughts and feelings as you either watched yourself and/or projected yourself into your past life. Note all the insights you received as you viewed who you were before and what you've experienced in your past life. Write down all the connections between your past and your present, and your understanding of how and why the memory you experienced can help you in your present life.

Exploring and Experiencing All Your Past Lives

You might want to explore and experience other past lives by projecting yourself into them. Take a mind trip around the world. Allow your higher self to guide you wherever you go. Visit and view many different countries, cultures, and civilizations where you feel you've lived before. (In addition to discovering your past lives through mind projection, you'll save a tremendous amount of money on airfare!)

After every trip, make detailed notes in your journal on everything you experience and become aware of. Include your thoughts and feelings about your trips, and all the images, insights, and information you receive. As you return to the present, bring with you all the knowledge you become aware of into your present life. Allow yourself to clearly understand how the events and emotions in your past lives relate to your present situations and feelings.

PART III

KARMA

13

Before Birth

In the interim between lives, you have complete understanding of all your experiences in every lifetime. This spiritual knowledge helps you choose and plan what you'll experience in your next lifetime. Before you reincarnate into your present life, you decide what goals you want to accomplish and what lessons you still need to learn. You choose how to balance your karma, and you decide what you're willing to experience. You choose the destiny you'll pursue and the path you'll follow in your life. Your choices and decisions are based on experiences in your previous lives—on how you feel about those past experiences, and by what you want to do about them in this life. You create the structure and framework, and form the foundation of your present life, supported by your experiences in previous lives and by your spiritual knowledge.

You plan and prepare the events for your next incarnation. You create the opportunities you want to experience and explore. You choose your companions, and set the stage for the experiences you'll share with them. You converse with souls in the spiritual realm, and you also communicate with souls who are experiencing a physical incarnation to confirm earlier choices made with them. You make promises and commitments, both to yourself and with other souls.

As you choose your experiences, you have access to all the spiritual knowledge you've gained throughout all your lifetimes, and you use that awareness to help you make your choices. Sometimes, you're assisted by guides and masters who offer advice on what might be best for you, but ultimately, the choice is yours. You create your circumstances; you set up your challenges; and you make connections by setting up synchronous occurrences on the earth plane.

Everything in your present life was created by you before birth. Nothing has been left to chance or forced upon you. The only thing you do not choose is the outcome of what you agree to experience. You make those choices and decisions, with your free will, when you're faced with those experiences in your present life.

You paint the picture of your present life on the canvas of creation and you color in the details. As you make your choices and decisions, the picture begins to take form, each character becoming clear, each event becoming more defined, and each experience becoming tangible and real. You create a masterpiece of mosaics that will fit together perfectly as your present life progresses. In a very real way, you create the world you'll experience in your upcoming incarnation.

When the timing and circumstances are right, you reincarnate into a physical body to put into practice the spiritual knowledge you've attained, and to follow through on your promises and commitments. The choices and decisions you've made become a memory and you retain a sense of them, on a subconscious level, where they innately guide you in the direction you've chosen by offering you the opportunities and challenges you've agreed to experience in this lifetime. As you experience your present life, you acquire even more spiritual wisdom as you learn lessons, balance karma, and fulfill your destiny.

ENTERING THE EARTH EXPERIENCE

Before birth, your soul exists as an energy vibration of awareness, knowledge, and light. As soon as you choose rebirth, you're committed and connected to your physical body in a spiritual way. Your soul can enter your body at any time from conception to three months after birth, and you have complete freedom of movement between the physical and the spiritual planes of existence until that time.

After the first three months of physical life, your soul becomes connected to your body until death do you part. Throughout your present incarnation, you retain the ability, through your inner knowledge, to travel through levels of awareness in a limited manner. You're restricted in the full awareness of your soul by choosing to express your spirituality on a physical level. This is known as the *veil of awareness*.

As you leave the spiritual realms and enter the earth experience, your soul assumes the physical energies that will enable you to exist in a physical environment. You experience this as a process of exchanging energies. At the moment of birth, there is a loss of awareness, due to the transition between spiritual and physical energies.

In reforming your energies by being born into the earth environment, you go through a transition of awareness as you travel through levels of energy. These vibrations range from the finest, highest energies, which represent your soul in spiritual form, to the more compacted and slower energies, which represent your consciousness in a physical body. Each of the levels of energy vibrates to a particular area of awareness, and you have different thoughts, feelings, and experiences in each expression of energy.

As you begin to leave the spiritual realm and travel through the levels of energy, light is all around you and within you, and you're completely aware of your soul. As you leave the atmosphere of spiritual awareness, you feel yourself floating through the energy vibrations of time, space, matter, and motion. As you experience the transition into the etheric level, you feel yourself moving through a cloud of light, which limits your awareness of your soul. As you pass through the veil of awareness, your spiritual wisdom begins to transform itself into a physical understanding of your soul.

As you begin to enter the earth environment, your transformed spiritual awareness enters your subconscious mind. You're aware of both the world you're leaving and the world you're entering. You're in the astral level, and you're balanced between spiritual and physical energies. You create a channel of communication between your spirituality and your physical awareness as you blend spiritual energies into physical energies.

As you begin to enter the energies of the earth environment, you feel your spiritual awareness and understanding become your inner truth and knowledge. As your soul begins to enter the body, you begin to adapt to physical energies. You're aware on a subconscious level and your thoughts are clear. You're aware that you've created the world you're entering, and you feel an anticipation of the experiences waiting for you.

As your soul connects with your body, you become fully aware of your physical body and earth energies. You feel a sense of the world around you, and you become aware of physical feelings. You complete the process of transition, and you experience a dense and heavy fog, which closes around you and closes you off from most of your spiritual energies. You feel a sense of confinement and limitation at first until you get used to being in physical form again. Welcome to the world.

14

The Law of Karma

Karma is a Sanskrit word meaning "action," and is most often referred to as cause and effect. Your actions from past lives are reflected in your experiences in your present life. The Law of Karma is also called the Law of Retribution, and has been mistakenly thought of as the negative events that happen to you that you seem to have no control over. Karma can be either positive or negative, depending on what you've done in your past lives. The good, the bad, the ugly, and the beautiful were all created by you. As you begin to understand and balance your karma, it's helpful to keep this in mind.

Since you're the one who created your karma, you're also the one who can change your karma. When you're balancing karma, you're correcting negative events and emotions by bringing them to a positive resolution. You're working with causes, either from past lives or from earlier in this life, that have resulted in present effects. By your thoughts, feelings, and actions—in both your past lives and your present life—you cause events to occur. You experience your karma through the effects of your previous thoughts, feelings, and actions, which are repercussions of the causes you set into motion. Karma surfaces when the time is right for balancing.

The Law of Karma is perfectly just and fair. You're the judge and the jury, and you determine your own sentence, based on your previous actions. If your karma seems unfair, you only have to look within yourself and your past-life memories to find out why. Karma is a constant law that's always in motion. If it seems unfair, you can change it by your thoughts, feelings, and actions in the present. As you accept responsibility for your karma, you give yourself the power to balance your karma.

You put the Law of Karma into effect with your free will. You create your karma and the way you experience it by your past attitudes and actions, and by your present reactions to the experiences you have. Free will is your choice of thoughts, feelings, actions, and responses in every experience and situation you encounter. By your free will, you either create karma or balance karma. You always have free will. It's your birthright.

You offer yourself many challenges and choices in the form of opportunities and experiences that will help you accomplish everything you've set out to do in your present life. Events in your life that you can't seem to change are events you predestined yourself to experience. Before birth you made an irrevocable agreement, either with yourself or with another soul, to participate in certain experiences. By committing yourself to the experience, you agreed to face the challenge. What you do when the challenge presents itself is determined by your free will. Fate is your free will surfacing in the present time and offering you the choice of following through or of not honoring the promises made before birth.

You create all the experiences in your life to learn lessons, to balance karma, to enjoy previous achievements, and for spiritual growth and the acquisition of knowledge. There are no such things as accidents, chance, or coincidence. If an accident occurs, it was done on purpose. Everything happens for a reason. The very nature of karma strives for balance.

CREATING YOUR OWN REALITY

Karma and free will walk hand in hand with creating your own reality. You create what you experience in every moment of every lifetime. Your present thoughts and feelings and the choices and decisions you make every day affect, influence, and change your experiences. You create your own reality through your present choices, and this affects both what you do about your karma and how you experience your karma.

Life can be as difficult or as easy, or as challenging and rewarding, as you create it and perceive it to be. You chose the earth experience to help you balance your karma in the most meaningful way possible. As you work with understanding and balancing your karma, don't limit yourself only to looking for past-life causes that are reflected in present effects. Also look to creating your own reality as a possible culprit that helps to perpetuate the negative experiences you encounter.

You can experience negative events in your life for any number of reasons. Although your past actions determine your present experiences, your current perceptions and feelings about your experiences determine how you react to them, whether they originated in your past lives or were created in the present. You can determine whether your experiences are from the past or the present by finding the underlying cause for your situation. Most often, especially if the situation is serious, the cause is karmic, aggravated by present perceptions and creations of negativity.

The difference between karma and creating your own reality is that karma was created in a past life and seems to be something mysterious that arises in the present out of a murky past to haunt you, while creating your own reality is what you do through your thoughts, feelings, and actions in the situations in your present life. When you created your karma in a past life, you were creating your own reality. In the present, as you create your own reality, you're creating karma that will surface either later in this lifetime or in a future life. Karma and creating your own reality are really one and the same, and are both governed by the universal law of cause and effect.

As you balance your karma, you create your own reality. Balancing your karma is experienced as a free-flowing movement that opens up your awareness of the truth as your previous actions and emotions unfold and reveal themselves in the present. Understanding what you did in your past lives offers you an interesting challenge and is one of the most enlightening parts of your journey. The inherent value of knowing what you did in your past lives comes full circle with the changes you can make now in your present life that will balance your karma and evolve your soul.

15

You and the People in Your Life

Your friends in the present have been companions in the past. The people you're close to, or are related to, shared previous lives with you, though they're probably in different roles this time. Your mother may have been your sister or your son, and your husband may have been your wife or a friend in a past life. You choose to be with people you've known before in various relationships to provide you with opportunities to balance karma with them or just to enjoy being with them again. When you meet them in this life, your soul remembers them and the events you've experienced with them in the past.

Your karma is interwoven with the relationships and experiences you have with people in your life. Many of your present relationships reflect past-life ties with people you've known before. If the relationship was negative in the past, you're together in this lifetime to correct the karma by balancing it and bringing it to a positive level. When you have problems with the people in your life or with the relationship, it's almost always due to negative karma that the two of you created with one another in a past life. If you've shared a positive relationship with them in the past, your bond is continued and enhanced in the present.

SOULMATES: THE SPECIAL PEOPLE

Friends and lovers you've shared previous lives with are soulmates. When you meet a soulmate, you feel an immediate connection and rapport with them, coupled with a sense of familiarity. You feel very comfortable with them, and the relationship you share is on a positive level. While you may experience some friction and a few problems, the negativity is easily resolved and, once understood, serves to help both of you learn an identical lesson. There are three different kinds of soulmates. Each has unique characteristics that make them unmistakable from other people in your life.

Companion soulmates are people who help you accomplish a goal, or help you fulfill a specific purpose. Their help can be a comment made in general conversation that sets you on the right path, or they may physically help you achieve a goal. They help you in various ways when you need it the most. They offer a mutual gift of learning, sharing, and helping. In a previous life, you've helped them and now they're returning the favor.

You meet companion soulmates every day in a variety of situations and circumstances. You recognize them as the friend who offers you perceptive advice about a problem, the acquaintance who offers you a ride when your car breaks down, or the teacher who inspires you to learn. He or she might be someone you have a common interest or hobby with who shares knowledge with you, or someone who encourages you to try something you want to do, or a boss who appreciates your work.

Companion soulmates are people you feel good about. They're people you've spent a brief time with in previous lives in a general way. There's usually no serious bond between you, and your present association with them tends to be short. If the bond between you becomes stronger due to positive and continued interactions in the present, they may become twin soulmates in the future.

Twin soulmates are people you've shared a special bond of

friendship with in many lifetimes. You feel completely natural and open with them. Meeting a twin soulmate is like running into a good friend you haven't seen for years. You immediately feel comfortable with this person and you pick up the relationship where it left off in a previous life, just as if there hasn't been any time lost between you. You recognize a twin soulmate as someone with all the characteristics of a companion soulmate, but with a much stronger bond between you.

Twin soulmates are usually close family members or special friends. Look at the really good friends you have who understand you completely, and you'll be looking at twin soulmates. Very often, you don't even need words to communicate with them because your souls are in tune on a telepathic level. You intuitively know their thoughts and feelings. You may also find that many experiences in your present life parallel those of your twin soulmate. Together, you help each other in many different ways to grow and learn, and your friendship becomes even stronger. Your present relationship usually lasts from several years to your entire lifetime. If you part company, you part in a positive way, and you value the friendship you've shared with them.

A *twin flame soulmate* is your one and only true soulmate. You've spent many lifetimes together, loving and caring about each other, and you share a deep spiritual bond. When you meet him or her again in this lifetime, you feel an instant attraction and a special rapport between you. It feels like there's an electric current of energy flowing between you, and you feel like you've known the person forever. Your soul instantly recognizes and remembers your twin flame soulmate, and you feel this on a very deep level within yourself.

You only have one true soulmate who is your perfect counterpart, and together you create a special kind of magic between you that you don't experience with anyone else in your life. A twin flame soulmate has all the characteristics and qualities of a companion and a twin soulmate combined into one person you feel very, very special about. This feeling is always equally reciprocal. It's been said that your twin flame soulmate is the other half of your soul, and together your souls form a complete union. When you find your twin flame soulmate, you've found your soul's mirror image. Your soul remembers the beauty and joy of the spiritual love you share, and seeks to experience and express this during your physical incarnations.

Your twin flame soulmate is most often of the opposite sex, although in some instances he or she can be a brother or a sister (usually a twin). You may even look like your soulmate, with identical features, especially around the eyes. An interesting phenomenon occurs between twin flame soulmates. Your spiritual energies are so in tune and connected with one another that there is an intertwined arc of energy between your auras. It looks like a rainbow joining your souls together.

Many people believe that once you've found your twin flame soulmate, you get married and live happily ever after. This is sometimes true, but you can experience problems because of negative karma incurred between you in previous lives. With a twin flame soulmate, there's always an undercurrent of love flowing between you that transcends any negativity.

You're not with your twin flame soulmate in every lifetime, because you each may have chosen to work on separate lessons, or to evolve your soul in an individual way. If you don't share a lifetime with them, you're still working toward being together by evolving your souls in a similar and spiritual way. You may be together for only a short time in any lifetime, because you may have agreed to help each other do something in a specific way, or you may be with them for your entire lifetime. It depends entirely on the agreements made between you before birth.

PAST-LIFE CONNECTIONS:
THE KARMIC TIE THAT BINDS

When you feel a connection with someone you meet for the first time, you've shared events and experiences with them in past lives, and you've either helped or hurt each other. There are other people in your life whom you're karmically tied to from previous lives. You may feel a strong attraction or an immediate dislike upon meeting them. You recognize them as a soul you're karmically connected with and not a soulmate. You have a sense or a feeling that something needs to be worked out and balanced between you.

There's always a reason for being together again in this lifetime, and that reason usually becomes apparent within a few days or weeks after meeting them. Your present relationship reflects the past-life tie. Whether the people in your life are soulmates or souls you're karmically connected to, they're in your life for a reason and a purpose. That purpose is either to enhance the relationship or to balance the karma shared between you, and sometimes is a combination of both.

Past-life emotions continue from lifetime to lifetime, and affect your relationships and feelings in successive lives. Many present problems have their origins in past lives. These problems, until they're resolved, continue to influence the present relationship and the experiences you share with a person. During a very traumatic past-life regression, Linda reexperienced her death scene from a previous life. "He's got a knife. He's going to kill me," she screamed in terror. "He's killed my children and now he's coming after me." Tears were streaming down her face as her body convulsed with the stabbing.

She had made the appointment for a past-life regression, hoping to discover the cause of her difficulties with her husband. She was seriously considering a divorce because of problems in the marriage and an uneasy feeling that her husband would physically harm her and their children. When she first met him in college, she experienced a strong feeling of fear. After meeting him, she became sick and had to go home. They began dating and she passed off her initial response to him as having had too much to drink.

After remembering what happened between them in a past life, Linda was able to understand her present feelings and gained many insights into both their past and present relationship. She realized they were replaying scenes that had occurred before, and she was determined to change this before it was repeated again. When she arrived home later that day, her husband said, "I killed you before and that's why we're having all these problems now." Even though he hadn't accompanied her to the regression, he remembered the same things. They separated for six months and now are together again, working through their shared karma with greater insight and understanding into both their past and present actions.

Your relationships can be a continuation of a previous relationship, and can reflect actions that were created and not balanced in the past. The relationship is in your life to repay karmic debts and for learning purposes. Amanda is an artist, and is also the mother of two young children. She has a studio at home and spends her days painting pictures, sandwiched between distractions from her children. She found herself becoming violent when they interrupted once too often.

She loves her children, and she's very dedicated to being an artist. She felt torn by the choice between her creativity and her children. In one past life with them, she had been too demanding and had kept her children from doing what they desired. In another past life, she had struggled to be an artist and didn't succeed. She realized she was experiencing the present situation to learn how to respect her children and their needs, and to overcome obstacles that had interfered with her painting in past lives.

Your relationships with friends and lovers may be a reversal of what you've done to them in past lives, and your personality may be a turnaround of what it was before. Donna and Doug had been dating for several months. He liked to go bar-hopping on weekends, and she preferred a quiet, intimate dinner. They compromised for awhile. They went out to dinner during the week, and went to bars on weekends. She hated going to bars, but went with him because she wanted to please him. She felt miserable about the relationship and felt that she couldn't communicate with him.

In a regression, Donna remembered several events from a past life they had shared where she hadn't cared about what he wanted and had dragged him into situations he didn't like. She had turned a deaf ear when he told her what he wanted. In this life, she was experiencing an identical reversal of what she had done to him in a past life. By not balancing the karma through resolving the present problem, they were both perpetuating the negativity and creating more karma between them that would have to be balanced, either later in this lifetime or in a future life.

"All's fair in love and war" may work on a negative level to help you achieve revenge, but it doesn't work on a spiritual level to help you balance your karma. What you do to another person, in a past life and in your present life, will come back to you, just like a boomerang, until it's resolved. If you manipulate another person, you'll find yourself being the puppet on a string next time. If you treat a person with respect, you'll be respected for it.

The karma you share with the people in your life can surface in many different ways. When you look at the situations you experience in your relationships, and you let your thoughts flow with how the present mirrors the past, you become aware of the past-life tie that binds you together. The reason you're with certain people at this time in your life is because the circumstances are most right for balancing the shared karma.

Opening-Up Exercises

As you balance karma with the people in your life, it is very helpful to completely understand it. Understanding your karma allows you to become aware of the past-life ties. Viewing your current relationship from an in-depth perspective will give you answers. By working with various levels of awareness, you can discover the karma to be balanced with another person. This gives you insights into the present problems and your responses to the relationship, and will help you see how the past and the present problems are intertwined and perpetuated.

Exercise 1. Think about someone in your life that you're experiencing problems with. In your journal, write down who the person is, the problem you're experiencing, and how it started in this life. Include your attitude toward and your emotions about this person. Write down what you feel the karma is that you need to balance with them and the reason they're in your life. This will give you insights into how you feel on a conscious level about the karma to be balanced, and will show you the surface negativity.

- To delve deeper into the karmic tie, enter an Alpha level and allow your higher self to guide you toward an understanding of how your present emotions and attitude color the feelings you have about the person and the shared karma. This will help you separate the past from the present and will help you get in touch with your true feelings. It will also reveal possible subconscious, and stubborn, blockages. In your journal, write down everything you become aware of. Note your true inner feelings about the person and the shared karma.

- To remember and become more clear on past-life causes that are mirrored in the present problem, enter an Alpha level and allow your higher self to guide you toward the lifetime where the problem began with this individual. Look at the part you both had in creating the shared karma. Look for any negative decisions and choices you made in the past about this relationship, and see how those previous decisions and choices are reflected in what you're experiencing now. Allow your higher self to give you insight and understanding into how and why this problem began in a past life. In your journal, write down everything you experience and become aware of.

- To discover why you're experiencing this problem in your life now, and to become aware of the agreements made before birth regarding this matter, enter an Alpha level and mind project into the interim between lives when you were preparing for this life and making decisions and choices with this person. Allow your higher self to guide you toward the awareness and understanding of the agreements and promises you made to each other, and to what experiences you both agreed to have in order to balance your shared karma. Be aware of the spiritual wisdom you had when you were creating the current circumstances you would share that would allow you to resolve the problem. In your journal, write down everything you experience and become aware of.

Exercise 2. Look over the notes you've written in your journal about everything you experienced and became aware of in your three-part meditation. The insights and information you've gathered will help you understand your current relationship and its origins in past-life events. It will give you answers into what you're experiencing now and why you're experiencing it. It will also help you understand why you've co-created and are participating in the present problem, and will help you determine whether you're ready to balance the shared karma.

To become aware of how you can balance the shared karma in the way that is most appropriate for you, enter an Alpha level and allow your higher self to show you ways to balance your karma in a positive way. In your journal, write down everything you become aware of.

All the notes you've written and all the insights and information you've booomo awaro of build tho baokground for undcrstanding and resolving the karma with the people in your life. The next two chapters offer more information on balancing karma.

16

Paying the IOUs from the Past

Balancing karma and learning life lessons complement each other, though they can be separate and distinct from one another. The lesson may need to be learned first before the karma can be balanced, or the karma may have to be balanced first in order to learn the lesson. Paying your IOUs from the past is experienced as a process that leads you through various levels of awareness and understanding into many different experiences, as the actions, reactions, and interactions from your past lives show themselves in the present.

Your experiences are stepping stones that enable you to get into the heart of the matter. The stepping stones are built from one experience that leads to other experiences. As you learn one lesson, or part of it, you move forward to learn the other parts of the lesson, or to step up to another lesson or to a new level of awareness. The steps connect and form a path that shows you the way to complete your lessons and balance your karma. The path you follow helps you understand the nature of your experiences and, in a symbolic way, the steps are your stairway to spirituality.

As you look at the present and you look within yourself to see the past, you'll uncover the basis for your present lesson or karma. You'll see all the steps you've taken that have led you to where you are now, and you'll see how your past experiences have formed your present experiences. By looking at your present situations, you'll become aware that you already intuitively know what needs to be done to balance the karma and learn the lesson.

Your emotions are a constant barometer of how you're striving to achieve balance. As you become aware of your karma, pay close attention to your feelings about the situations and relationships you're involved in. Notice your motives and underlying reasons *why* you react the way you do to the events in your life. Your feelings will show you what the lesson is and what you need to do to balance the karma.

UNDERSTANDING YOUR KARMA

There are varying degrees and shades of gray in understanding your karma. Easy answers are the exception, not the rule. Some things in your life may be downright difficult to achieve or understand. Don't let this dampen your spirits. You've been learning life lessons and balancing karma since the beginning of time, but you probably called it common sense, or good, clean living, or following your instincts before you started calling it karma and balancing. Although it's true that by learning the lesson and balancing the karma, you're done with it, the opposite of that is also very true. You may find that once you understand what the lesson is, the situation remains in your life because that, in itself, is the lesson or karma.

For example, let's say that you're blind in this lifetime. In a past life, you caused someone else to be blind. After all, an eye for an eye seems fair. In a different past life, you looked down on other people. You set up your karma this time as a two-part payback. The karma is to experience being blind, and the lesson to learn is to see how your previous actions and attitudes have hurt other people. However, just because you've understood your karma and experienced being blind and you've learned from it, doesn't necessarily mean your eyesight will be miraculously restored (although it can and does happen).

The manner in which you pay back your karma and learn your lessons was determined by you before birth. You created the perfect circumstances and situations that would enable you to balance your karma and learn your lessons in the way that is most right for you. Once you've corrected the negativity from the past and learned from it in the present, you've balanced your karma. You'll reap the rewards later in this life or in your next lifetime, depending on what the lesson and karma is, and on what you've agreed to experience.

Don't breathe a sigh of relief just yet. If you balance your karma because you want to get it over with, or because you never want to experience it again, then you haven't really balanced it. You've only postponed it, and you've probably made it worse. If you build up blame, anger, resentment, hostility, or any other negative feelings while you're supposed to be learning and balancing, you'll have to do it all over again until you get it right.

There are a few twists and turns in the process of balancing karma and learning life lessons. Experiencing your karma isn't enough. You have to balance it and learn from it, too. If you don't balance it, then all you've done is subjected yourself to a negative experience that you're destined to experience again. Just because you suffer through the karma doesn't mean it's balanced. It only means you've suffered through the experience without learning the lesson by not understanding and resolving the negativity.

Your past attitudes and actions have created the circumstances and situations in your life. Your feelings determine the manner in which you're tied to your experiences and connected with other people. The karma you're experiencing is due to your actions and emotions in past lives, and is joined with how you respond to your present situations. Look carefully at your experiences to determine the previous choices and emotions that put them into action. Decisions made in past lives, especially ones made while feeling extremely emotional, also govern what you experience. Your past choices can either help you move forward or can cause you to get stuck in negative patterns.

Watch out for situations in your life that appear to be positive on the surface. The positive could be a disguise for the negative underneath the situation. Beware the "always" syndrome. In a past life, you may have achieved something wonderful and decided that you always wanted to do this one particular thing. Because of this decision, you're limiting your opportunities in the future and tying yourself to always doing the same thing, instead of growing from your original experience. Your feelings, which formed the past decision, come from a desire to continue something positive that you're done with. If you hang onto something once you're finished with it, you only hurt yourself and possibly others, and you prevent yourself from enjoying what you've accomplished. You can experience the results of this decision in the present by feeling obligated to do something that you feel holds you back now.

On the other hand, the opposite is also true. It depends on how you perceive the situation. You could be experiencing a positive situation that appears to be negative. In the process of balancing your karma, the positive permeates through the negative and becomes the end result. For example, in your present life, you could be involved in a situation that you feel trapped in. Because of the very nature of the situation and your feelings about it, the situation becomes an experience that leads you forward and allows you to expand and grow into another area you wouldn't have been able to explore if you hadn't felt trapped and compelled to change the situation.

Be on guard for decisions you've made about another person. In past lives, you may have decided that you always wanted to be with a certain person. Because of that decision, you could be holding yourself back, as well as the other person by infringing upon his or her free will and tying yourself to that person, perhaps in a negative way through guilt or blame. Your decision is based on a fear of change and a desire to keep the relationship the same. Your feelings constrict the flow of positive energy in your present life and limit the positive aspects of the experience. Instead of enjoying a relationship that becomes even better, this decision causes you to move backward and turns the relationship into a negative experience. This also creates karma with this person that will have to be balanced in the future.

Beware the "never" syndrome. In a past life, you may have decided that you'll never do something again, or that a particular event will never happen to you again. Because of this decision, you're carrying over unresolved emotions and you're asking to repeat the lesson. You could be trying to avoid a dreaded ordeal, instead of experiencing it and learning from it. Your feelings, which precipitated your decision, come from an underlying fear that originated from a negative experience, and this fear condemns you to reexperience the situation. In going through it again, you'll find that it becomes worse than it was before.

You can experience your karma as strong emotional feelings, either with or without the corresponding past-life memory. Sometimes the emotion survives very strongly while the memory is repressed, due to its painful or traumatic nature. Ted feels anxiety and an unidentifiable fear when he goes to work and leaves his family at home. When he's with them, he feels overprotective and possessive. In a previous life, he was injured while hunting for food for his family, and died before he could get back to them. Circumstances prevented him from providing for his family, and they starved to death.

His family now is the same one as before, and he constantly worries about being able to provide food for them. He carries large amounts of life insurance, as well as an overwhelming sense of guilt and responsibility. He feels he failed them before and is now trying to prove he can take care of them. He doesn't want his wife to work because he feels she should stay at home and take care of their children. She wants to work to be able to take care of herself and to help support the family.

It seems likely that he vowed to take care of them this time, promising himself that the past-life experience would never happen again. On the surface, this appears to be a very honorable decision, but look underneath the current situation. In that past life, his family didn't become helpless victims. They had chosen that experience to learn how to rely on themselves. By not learning their lesson in the past, they helped to perpetuate the present situation.

As Ted tries to balance his karma in this way, by allaying the guilt he felt before instead of resolving it, he's in the process of building up anger and resentment. The friction created by his wife pursuing her own career, coupled with his feelings about being able to take care of his family, increases the negativity. These feelings will surface, both in the present and in a future life, as they become destined to play out the past and present karma until it's resolved in a positive way.

Sometimes the positives are so mixed up with the negatives that it's hard to tell where one leaves off and the other begins. As you balance your karma, it's important to be clear on what your karma is, and not carry it to an extreme or overcompensate for it in the present. You only want to balance your karma, not create more. The whole idea is to find the balance, or the middle point, and then resolve the negatives. Once it's resolved, you can either let go of it entirely or improve on the positives, depending on the situation. Gauge your feelings in relation to the present situation to determine if your reactions are appropriate. Your feelings will help you understand and resolve your karma.

There are many perils and pitfalls involved in carrying over unresolved negative emotions into your present life. The negativity, until it's resolved, will continue to rear its ugly little head in your experiences, and will influence and affect your actions and feelings. Negative past-life decisions and the emotions that originated them are very damaging in the present. Feelings of guilt, resentment, fear, and anger from a past life can cause physical and emotional repercussions in your present life, and can show themselves in many negative ways. All those nasty, terrible things that haunt you and hurt you also prevent you from fully balancing your karma, while they lock you into negative experiences.

When you carry over past-life emotions because you misunderstand your lesson, or because you feel you need to suffer in order to repay karma, you're only hurting yourself by condemning yourself to a negative experience that there's no need for. Don't do this to yourself. You don't deserve it. You're not balancing karma; you're only punishing yourself, and perhaps building up negative feelings that will surface in a future lifetime, making your karma even more difficult to repay. Sometimes, you can dig yourself in so deep that it requires a superhuman effort to get yourself out.

While you may need to experience some negativity in order to learn the lesson and balance your karma, it serves several purposes. The negativity gets your attention and helps to make you aware of what you did in the past. It allows you to experience it in the present in order to understand it better. Most important, it provides you with the awareness and knowledge of how to truly learn the lesson and balance your karma.

Karma doesn't have to be a painful process. It can be a very beautiful experience as it becomes an awareness of the truth. Remembering and understanding events and emotions from your past lives helps you to know the justice in what you're experiencing. Through balancing your karma and learning your life lessons, you acquire the wisdom and understanding that evolves your soul.

IDENTIFYING KEY ISSUES AND PAST-LIFE INFLUENCES

Events and emotions from your past lives both directly and indirectly influence the situations and circumstances in your present life. You can become aware of the life lessons you chose this time by the way your life is going, and by how you feel about key issues in your life. By taking a good, honest look at the things that are important to you and the things you feel strongly about, you can become aware of the lessons and your karma within your experiences and feelings.

Negative issues are very indicative of lessons to be learned and karma to be balanced. When you look at the opposite side of the negative issues you're facing, you'll see what the lesson is. For example, if you're very possessive about everything in your life, then your lesson is to learn how to let go and to be more accepting. The connecting karma could be a payback for being overly possessive in a past life, or it could be the playing out of a fear of having something taken away from you, which may have occurred before. If you're very impatient and you want everything yesterday, then your lesson is patience. The karma could involve a past life where you were lazy and didn't accomplish anything, or it could involve a life where you weren't able to achieve your goals, and in this lifetime you're overcompensating.

Many people struggle with a lack of money, and it seems that everything they do to earn money is unsuccessful. If you don't have enough money, or if you're barely making ends meet, you could have had money in a previous life and misused it, or the trials and tribulations you experience because of lack of money can be due to a karmic situation you chose to balance in this way for any number of reasons. You could be struggling to support a family because you deserted them in a previous life. You could have created these circumstances to learn how to share, or to be honest, or to become aware of important values in life, or because you want the experience of being poor to learn how to earn and enjoy money.

Your circumstances can also be due to factors in your present life. You could be responding to earlier negative programming that led you to believe being poor was all you could expect. Your parents may have been poor, and you accepted this way of life for yourself. You could also be buying into limiting beliefs about being unsuccessful, or a fear of always having to struggle to earn a living. And, because you believe it, this creates what you experience.

Your present circumstances offer you the opportunity to reevaluate your current beliefs and to learn the lesson and balance your karma by making positive changes. Once you've learned the lesson, or changed your feelings about your situation, you'll have money again, and it will reflect the lesson learned and the karma that was balanced by mirroring the positive changes you've made. In addition to being the reward, it will also be a test to see if you've learned the lesson and truly changed your feelings.

Look at your fears. The things you're afraid of will show you what you want to overcome. In understanding and resolving your fears, you learn the lesson. For example, if you're afraid of being alone, or if you're lonely and don't have many friends, then the lesson could be to learn independence. The karma could be a payback for being too dependent or too demanding on other people in a past life. As you balance your karma, you overcome your fear by accepting it and experiencing it. This enables you to learn the lesson, and allows you to make positive changes.

You can learn your lessons without directly experiencing the effects of your karma. If you feel connected to or participate in someone else's experience, even as an outside observer, there's a lesson in it for you that you chose to learn in this particular manner. For example, if you have a friend who experiences a traumatic or painful event in his or her life, you may feel the repercussions of that situation in your life. If you become involved by helping or sympathizing with your friend, you're participating in the experience to the extent that you're feeling your friend's emotions within your own feelings, sometimes just as much as if you were going through the experience yourself.

Karma continues from lifetime to lifetime. Serious issues are indicative of karma that has been continued and carried over into several lifetimes. You may choose not to balance the karma, or you may not be able to balance all the karma in your present life, because of the unavailability of required circumstances. Sometimes, the many varied aspects and expressions of your karma can only be partly balanced in this lifetime. The karma may have to be continued into a future life where you'll have the opportunity to fully experience the effects of your actions, and where the circumstances will enable you to complete the balancing.

Identifying key issues and recognizing past-life influences are only the tip of the iceberg. What's underneath the surface is what's really important. To get in touch with the deeper issues, begin by looking at the way they manifest in your present life. Oversimplify the issues to the point where you can see the central theme in a condensed form. It can be overwhelming if you try to see all the ramifications at once.

You can do more than just scratch the surface. When you have a clear view of what the present situation is, look below the surface to find the underlying cause or causes. Open up and explore your thoughts and feelings about how the past influences and affects the present. Notice how your present feelings and experiences are connected with the past-life cause. Even insignificant and seemingly unrelated events can play a major role. There can be many lessons involved in one issue, and many influences from different past lives that are related to your present karma.

Opening-Up Exercises

You can identify your key issues and their influence by looking in your present life. Karma reveals itself through current challenges, and is reflected in your feelings and experiences. Situations or feelings you repeatedly encounter are the replaying of a pattern or an influence from a past-life event that is not yet balanced. You can determine the past-life causes and the emotions, actions, lessons, and karma that you carry over by looking into your present situations and your feelings.

Exercise 1. In your journal, make a list of several situations you're currently experiencing that indicate a past-life event or emotion is being carried over and continued in your present life. Your list can show your attitude or your emotions, or represent things you do on a consistent basis. From your list, choose the one situation that is most important to you right now. Write down how it began in this life, and what precipitated its occurrence. Identify all the elements and the emotions involved. Note all your present feelings about it.

To begin with, look objectively at your present situation. It can be easier to look at serious issues if you take yourself out of them. This allows you to clearly see the situation and to offer yourself advice, while you acquire insights and gain tremendous understanding. This helps you see how you feel about the situation on a surface level, and will show you how the past event is manifested in your present life, and how your past emotions influence your present feelings. This also helps you go within the situation and get in touch with your true feelings about it in a more open way.

Once you become aware of the influence from a past-life event and how you feel about it, you can delve more deeply into it to find the past-life cause and to see its present and future effects. You can explore your current situation further by watching a three-part movie of your past, present, and future lives. [See Chapter 12, "Projecting Yourself into Your Past Lives" and "Mind-Tripping into Your Memories."] As you watch and experience the movie, you'll follow the current situation and its effect in your present life as it leads you to the origin of the appropriate past-life cause, and shows you the present repercussions and future manifestations of your situation.

The Past: The situation you choose to work with will be the title of your movie, and your notes about the situation will form the background for your movie. Enter an Alpha level and create an image that symbolizes the present situation which includes and shows all your current feelings about it. This is the opening scene in your past-life movie. Your movie begins in the present with your current situation and the way it began in this life, and then flashes back to scenes from a past life. Your movie will show you the past-life origin of the present situation. Pay attention to your feelings as you're watching the movie. Allow your higher self to be your commentator and your guide, and to explain how and why the situation was created, perpetuated, and carried over into your present life.

Watch the movie as the scenes portray the actions of what you did, and show you the events you experienced in a past life. Watch how the plot thickens, and notice all the interactions between the characters and the situations in your movie, and how it all relates to your present situation. If you feel comfortable with it, project yourself into the movie, so you're experiencing it as well as watching it. Your feelings will help you become aware of many more details that bring up clear and intense memories. Explore and experience all the images, events, and emotions you see and feel in your movie. Discover all you want to know about your past-life experiences and emotions that caused and created your present situation.

In your journal, write down everything you experienced in your past-life movie. Include the title, the opening scene, and the flashbacks. Note all your past and present feelings, and the images you saw and experienced. Write down all your observations about the movie. Make connections with the information offered in the movie to the past-life cause of your current situation and its influence and the effects in your present life. (If you're not sure, ask your higher self for the answer.) This will help you understand why you're experiencing the situation in your life now, and will show you exactly what the lesson and the karma is.

(Note: You may find that the issue you're working with also surfaces in your dreams. As you look more deeply into the karmic aspects of your situation, the dreams may become lucid dreams. [See Chapter 10, "Discovering Your Past Lives Through Your Dreams."])

The Present: Once you understand the past-life origin of your present situation, and you're aware of what the lesson and the karma is, watch the second part of the movie to see the natural progression of events in the present that will correct the situation and resolve the negativity. The movie will show you the choices and decisions you've made in this lifetime and before birth, and how you created your present situation in order to complete your karma.

Watch the movie as it shows you how to learn the lesson and balance your karma. This part of the movie begins in the present and advances into the near future. It shows you the positive changes in action as they affect and influence your present situation, and how the changes will play out in your life. This offers you many insights into how and why you've created your present situation and also shows you where you're going with it, based on your prebirth choices and your present feelings about it.

In your journal, write down the changes you saw that will enable you to learn the lesson and balance your karma in the present. Note all your feelings about resolving the issue, and pay particular attention to the present and future images you saw in this part of the movie. This shows you that you already know how to learn the lesson and balance your karma. Your movie also previews the effects of your positive resolutions in the future in this lifetime—if you choose to put them into motion.

The Future: Past and present events and emotions—if they remain unresolved—will continue to influence and affect you, and will govern your experiences, both in this lifetime and in your future lives. Just to see what happens to your current situation if you don't learn the lesson and balance the karma, and you continue it into the future, create another version of the movie to see how your present situation will influence your experiences later in this lifetime and in future lives. Watch the movie as it shows you the effects of your current situation in the future if no changes are made in the present.

In your journal, write down everything you become aware of about the unchanged situation in your present life that is carried forward. Note all the images you saw, and your feelings about how the situation plays out in the future. (Note: The future is malleable and impressionable. What you saw in this part of your movie is not etched into stone. Keep in mind that what you do in the present will affect and alter what occurs in the future. You're only looking at how the future will manifest if no changes are put into effect in the present.)

Changing and Creating Your Own Reality: If you want to see how different choices and changes you make in the present will be reflected in the future, you can reframe this particular part of the movie. This helps you decide if, how, and when you want to balance your karma (as seen in the second part of the movie), and the best way to do it, by giving you a preview of what can happen in the future with the various choices and changes you make in the present.

This part of the movie, if you watch it closely, will show you the art of creation, on a beginning level, as it follows the law of probabilities, with its basis in your present choices. This will open up many avenues for you to explore, and will show you how you create your experiences through your feelings, beliefs, and free will. It offers you insights and knowledge into creating your own reality by showing you how your thoughts become tangible.

This is similar to what you do in the spiritual realm as you create your present incarnation. Before birth, you have a much broader picture and a much clearer perspective, and you're working with higher levels of knowledge, awareness, and understanding as you're creating your life, but with less control than you have in the physical realm. This is because your choices solidify themselves with the energies of your thoughts, and are influenced to a great extent by your current feelings and your free will.

(Note: Watch this part of the movie as an objective observer; *not* as a participant. If you become involved, through your feelings, you'll be putting your energy into motion and you'll be creating what you're seeing. Once you energize your choices, they'll manifest in the manner you create them, and will remain in effect until you change them again. If you decide to put what you're seeing into motion, then provide it with lots of positive energy by surrounding it with white light.)

On a sky-blue background, project a variety of choices and changes about your current situation; then choose the ones you like best. (The energy vibrations of the color blue in the background will contain the energies of your choices until you're ready to manifest them.) Watch the movie to see how the changes—*if* you were to make them—would play out in your present life. Allow your higher self to show you all the repercussions of the actions in motion, by seeing their effects before the causes are actually created. Notice how the movie changes and forms different pictures as you project your various choices. The film becomes a fluid movement, synchronized and flowing with your thoughts.

In your journal, record all your observations about the choices and changes you can create in the present. Write down how this part of the movie presented itself as you saw the changes occurring, and how the picture changed as your thoughts changed. Note how you felt about each of your choices as they showed themselves manifesting in your life. Write down your perceptions about how you create your own reality. This will help you accept responsibility for your current karma and will also help you discover the power you have to balance it in your present life.

Exercise 2. After viewing your movie and gaining insights and answers into your present problem, work on resolving the present situation in the way that is most appropriate for you. As you make positive changes in the present, write detailed notes in your journal. Keep a daily diary of your thoughts and feelings. Notice how your actions have caused reactions, and note what you're doing to change the current situation and what still needs to be done. As you work on making the positive changes, putting them into action, and seeing their effects, you'll become aware of how to perfectly resolve the negativity by learning the lesson and balancing any karma that remains. [Also see Chapter 17.]

THE BENEFITS OF BALANCING

Although getting back to the past-life cause enables you to understand the present-life effect better, it's not absolutely necessary. You can learn the lesson and balance your karma in the present without remembering the specific event from the past. The events from your past lives are reflected in the present. Once you correct the present situation and have positive feelings about it, you've balanced the past.

One of the benefits of experiencing and balancing karma is the many doorways it can open for you. When you're faced with negative karma, look inside it to see all the positive potentials and all the benefits you're acquiring from having the experience. Sometimes your worst experiences turn into the very best things that could ever have happened to you.

By coping with and coming to terms with your karma, you can learn the positives from experiencing the negatives. Sally was an abused child, who spent most of her young life being black and blue and bloody. To survive emotionally, she lived in her imagination. By going within herself, she grew up to be a wonderfully creative and imaginative writer. By being unloved and neglected, she learned how to love herself and how to depend on herself. She balanced her karma with the abusive parent and, in the various stages of learning her lesson, fully developed her creative abilities.

Present situations reflect similar past-life situations, and they can also be a reversal of the past situation. The lesson from the past is mirrored in the present. Celia was pressured by her parents to become a real estate agent. She trained for it, obtained her license, and hated every minute of it. When she got in touch with her feelings about why she didn't want to sell houses, she remembered a past life where she had been a landlord and had run out the families that couldn't pay.

In making the connection with the past-life memory, she realized she still had strong feelings of guilt about displacing people from their homes. By selling houses in this lifetime, she triggered into her previous feelings about forcing people to leave their homes. Through understanding the past-life cause of her present feelings, she was able to let go of the guilt by realizing that now she was helping people to find homes. She recognized that she had balanced her karma, and felt free to change careers and pursue her lifelong dream of becoming a veterinarian.

Once you've learned a lesson or balanced karma, or acquired a skill or talent, you enjoy the benefits of what you've earned and accomplished through your efforts in previous lives. While you may not be directly aware of the influence in the present, you can experience your past achievements in many positive ways. They may surface as a career you feel completely fulfilled in, or as a natural talent or flair for doing something. You may also experience the benefits of balancing as a wonderful relationship you share with someone, or as positive traits and qualities you possess.

Your present achievements and accomplishments can be something you've worked for and earned in many lifetimes, which you've carried over into the present, and are a reward for what you've learned and balanced in previous lives. This holds true for lessons that are nearly completed. You may have begun them in past lives and continued them into the present. A completion is always positive and shows the lesson is completely learned and the karma is perfectly balanced. Learning your lessons and balancing your karma allows you to move forward in your life, to explore new areas and experiences, and to evolve on both a physical and a spiritual level.

Opening-Up Exercise

Your accomplishments will show you how you're enjoying the benefits of balancing. In your journal, make a list of achievements and/or issues you've already resolved. Choose the achievement you're most proud of, or the situation that feels most complete. See how you've carried it forward by looking into your past lives to find the origin and the connecting links to the present. Enter an Alpha level and allow your higher self to show you how you've balanced the karma and learned the lesson, and how you're reaping the rewards.

In your journal, write down what you experienced and became aware of as you saw how you've carried your achievement or the situation forward, and how you've balanced your karma. Note your efforts and experiences in every lifetime that brought it to completion in this lifetime. Write down how it influences and affects your present life, and how you experience it.

This meditation will help you realize how you've balanced your karma and brought it to a perfect resolution by showing you the unique way you process a completion through various experiences in several lifetimes. It shows you the path you've followed and your stepping stones to successfully completing your karma. It helps you become aware of choices and decisions you've made that affected what you experienced with your karma.

Your achievements offer you a blueprint of your attitudes and actions, showing you their cause and effect, and how the Law of Karma and creating your own reality operates. With the understanding you receive, you'll become aware that—through your free will—you are the director of your destiny and the master of your fate.

17

Balancing Your Karma

Balancing your karma is very important to your soul's evolvement and your spiritual growth. It's one of the main reasons you chose the earth experience. As you evolve your soul through the process of your physical incarnations, you must experience all aspects of your experiences and feelings in order to obtain a complete understanding. For example, to experience what love is, you must also experience hate. To know what wisdom is, you also have to know what ignorance is. There are two sides to everything; one cannot exist without the other; and they cannot coexist in harmony. This forms a foundation of existence and balance in which all things are created and manifested.

There's more to balancing karma than just correcting the mistakes and resolving the negative events and emotions you incurred in your past lives. By understanding the balance between all things, you learn and grow spiritually, and this frees you from the earth experience as it opens other doorways into higher realms of evolvement and knowledge. As you balance your karma through your experiences, you purify your soul and you raise your level of awareness. This is an important step on your path that leads you toward enlightenment.

Everything in nature and the physical realm is governed by the universal Law of Balance. You can see this in the rising and setting of the sun, the changing of the seasons, the phases of the moon, and the ebb and flow of ocean tides. The Law of Balance in nature is manifested in rhythms and patterns that follow a natural order and flow of energy in a cycle of harmony. Balance is energy in motion. Karma is action and reaction. Due to interactions between positive and negative energies in the experiences you have, karma leads to movement and change. The Law of Balance is manifested in the physical realm by changes you make in your life because of your experiences.

Your soul follows the Law of Balance, with cycles of birth and death, or rhythms of reincarnation. Your soul is composed of spiritual vibrations of energy, and you have the ability and the power to influence and change various forms of physical energy through your feelings, thoughts, and actions. The positive actions you employ within your experiences enable you to achieve balance and harmony. By balancing your karma and understanding your experiences, you also balance your physical nature with your spiritual nature. You gain knowledge and you harmonize the energies of your soul. This allows you to express your spiritual nature within your experiences.

In the process of balancing your karma, you receive an understanding of both the physical and spiritual nature of all your experiences by seeing the many aspects of everything you're involved in. Through this, you achieve understanding and insight that bring about positive resolutions and changes, resulting in inner peace and harmony. In achieving balance, you have a center point from which to express yourself in the manner you choose. Ideally, you earn and acquire wisdom and enlightenment, and you perfect your soul.

THE PROCESS OF POSITIVE CHANGE

Balancing your karma is accomplished by completely learning the lessons involved, and by making changes in your life that reflect the balancing. It's up to you to choose how to balance your karma. No one knows better than you what to do. Your circumstances are unique to you, and you must decide if, how, and when you'll balance your karma.

The crux of karma is what you choose to do about it. The crosses you bear by not balancing your karma become heavy burdens that weigh you down and prevent you from moving forward. If you choose to keep yourself tied to negative karma, it will continue to influence and affect you, as it offers you opportunities to balance. If you balance your karma through positive efforts and changes, you'll gain knowledge and enjoy all the benefits of balancing, as you free yourself to move forward in your life.

As you uncover and understand the past-life cause of your current karma, you become aware of your responsibility in originating your karma. Getting back to the cause helps you understand the present situation and offers you a wealth of information. By accepting your karma, you give yourself the power to make positive changes, which balance your karma. The best and most opportune time to balance your karma is when it presents itself. This is because your emotions and past-life memories are close to the surface and they enable you to get into the heart of the karmic situation.

Balancing karma occurs through a natural process of positive change, and begins with your desire to change. This is the first step in balancing. The second step is understanding both your past and present emotions and the events involved in what you want to balance, and knowing why you want to achieve balance. The third step is changing and reframing your feelings and perceptions about both the present and the corresponding past-life events and emotions, by seeing the positive aspects of the experience and deciding what you want to do about it. The fourth step is the efforts and actions you take to balance your karma. Understanding and balancing your karma is experienced as a fluid process that occurs automatically as your desire to change sets it into motion. You can see the results of this process by how the positive changes manifest in your life.

As you balance your karma, changes occur in your life that reflect the balancing, both on an inner and an outer level. One of the most important changes you can make is in your thoughts and feelings about the karma to be balanced. By looking at the present in a positive way, you begin to change your feelings and perceptions. As you change your feelings in the present, the energy surrounding the connecting past-life event changes. Reframing your perceptions of past-life events and the present effects caused by them consists of looking at what you've learned and the benefits you've gained by having the experience.

As you do this, you influence and affect the energy manifestation of your karma, and the negativity is resolved through your understanding. By making positive changes in your life, you complete the process of balancing and the negative event becomes a positive event, because you perceive it in a positive way. The event itself doesn't change, but your attitude does, and this is what changes the energy around past-life events. That energy then begins to manifest in positive ways that are reflected in your present life.

As you balance your karma, you may need to do it in small steps rather than in one giant leap. Balancing begins within your mind, and is expressed first through your positive thoughts and feelings. As you change and reframe your feelings and perceptions about the events and emotions from the past, and their corresponding effects in the present, it's important to put your thoughts and feelings into action. As you balance your karma by putting positive changes into motion, you begin to see those changes reflected in your experiences. Balancing is a process that occurs in stages, and it takes time for the results to fully manifest themselves. This becomes a rewarding and enriching experience as you watch your progress as you move forward.

Positive effort always results in positive changes. Positive changes occur in direct proportion to positive action. By your positive actions, you create a chain reaction that is truly awesome and powerful. As you balance your karma by bringing it to a positive level, the negativity is neutralized through your actions to enhance the positive. The positive then grows and expands from the center point of balance, leading you to higher levels of awareness and into other experiences. This allows you to move forward in your life and in your spiritual evolvement.

In the process of balancing your karma and putting your energy into motion, the change is incorporated into your lifestyle. As you live the change, you direct energy in the form of your thoughts, feelings, and actions in the direction you've decided to pursue. It's very important to balance in a positive way by moving toward what you want, rather than moving away from what you don't want. On first glance, the above statement may appear to say the same thing; the distinction is very subtle, but it makes a world of difference.

If you're moving away from what you don't want, you're directing your energy in a negative way. Your results will follow the flow of your energy. If you choose to balance your karma in a negative way, or for the wrong reasons, you'll find that the negative is what you end up with. For example, let's say the karma you want to balance involves an unhappy relationship. You dump the relationship by walking away from it. For a time, it appears that you're done with it, even though this leaves you with bad feelings about it. Because of your feelings, and by not resolving the negativity, you find your next relationship becomes the same as your original relationship. By moving away from what you don't want, you get what you wanted to get rid of.

When you move toward what you want, you direct your energy in a positive way and you experience positive results. You begin to balance your karma by understanding your feelings about what you want to change in the relationship and why you want to change it. You then change your thoughts and feelings to reflect what you want, and you decide whether to keep the relationship or let it go. If you keep it, you put positive changes into action. If you let it go, you do it in a positive manner. Either way, this provides you with good feelings about it, and you've allowed yourself to grow and learn from the experience. When you balance in this way, you're moving toward what you want, and you're receiving all the positive benefits of balancing.

PRINCIPLE OF FORGIVENESS

You can employ the principle of forgiveness to help you balance your karma. This is sometimes difficult to accomplish, because you may need to face—very honestly and directly—some awful things you've done in the past, or some awful things other people have done to you. This is part of the process of understanding and changing your feelings, and then reframing your perceptions by seeing the positive aspects of the experience. To balance your karma with the principle of forgiveness, you either forgive yourself or the other person, according to what the situation warrants. In many situations, you need to forgive both yourself and the other person.

Forgiveness, to be effective, needs to be done sincerely through your feelings and from your soul. This doesn't mean you have to say you're sorry. "Sorry" is a wretched word implying that blame, regrets, self-recrimination, and other negative feelings are still being held. Forgiveness means you've changed all your negative feelings into positive feelings, and is expressed through the actions you take to balance your karma.

The principle of forgiveness works by accepting and understanding the negativity you've incurred and experienced in your past lives, and then by changing that negativity, through your thoughts and actions, into a positive reflection of how you truly feel. The karma, consisting of your experiences, feelings, and inherent lessons, has been completely understood and learned. When the principle of forgiveness is sincerely applied, your karma is balanced. The results begin to show themselves immediately, first through your feelings, and then through the positive changes you see in your life.

PRINCIPLE OF GRACE

Another way to balance karma is through the principle of grace. You erase the need for negative karma to occur, because you supersede the occurrence of circumstances that would offer you the opportunity to balance. You apply the principle of grace through your positive actions and by your attitude. This is a continuous day-to-day action, which affects everything you do in a particular area of your life. You live the principle of grace and it becomes a blanket balancing. A blanket balancing is general in nature and encompasses a wide area of related feelings and situations.

To apply the principle of grace, you have to be aware of what you want to balance in a general way. You don't need to know the specifics of your karma; just be in touch with your feelings about it. The lesson you feel you need to learn will determine what you do in "gracing" yourself. For example, if one of your lessons is to learn how to be more tolerant of other people and their actions, you would employ the principle of grace by being more accepting of people in every situation in your life.

The principle of grace can also soften any negativity you choose to experience. For example, let's say you caused someone to be crippled in a past life. In this life, you need to experience being crippled as part of balancing your karma. Let's also say you're actively involved in working with a charity that helps people who are crippled. By helping and caring for others in this way, and by achieving empathy and compassion, you're superseding the experience of being crippled. Your karma could be softened by breaking both of your legs in a skiing accident. You still experience the effect of not being able to walk, and you learn and understand what being crippled is like, but it's only for a short time, instead of an entire lifetime.

The principle of grace has a ripple effect, which expands as it influences everything it touches. It's just like throwing a stone into a pond. It begins with one ripple, and spreads out to an innumerable quantity of joined, yet separate ripples. It sometimes takes longer to balance in this way, and the rewards are highly diversified, as the results are reflected in a wider and more far-reaching manner. One of the best ripple effects of the principle of grace is that it helps you perfect your soul in every aspect of your life you choose to apply it in.

SHARED KARMA

At times, your karma is so interwoven with situations and people in your life that it can be difficult to know whether the karma is shared with another soul or separate. Balancing karma that involves another person is different from balancing karma that relates to you individually, because there's more than just your soul and your free will involved. You're working with another person and their free will; that person is also making choices about whether to balance or not balance the karma you share.

When you're working with shared karma, you only have the right to make choices for yourself. You cannot infringe upon another person's free will or force them to balance. To do so would incur serious negative karma. An important thing to be aware of is that you only have to clear up your part of the karma. You're then released from it and freed from the experience. You don't have to be tied to a situation or a relationship by waiting for someone else to be ready to balance before you can complete your karma. You're only responsible for you. No one can hold you back if you choose to move forward.

There are two ways to balance shared karma with another person. If you both choose to balance, you can work through the karma together. Most often, balancing is an unspoken agreement and occurs by interactions with the other person. If he or she chooses not to balance, you can still balance your part of the karma. The other person isn't directly involved in the balancing process, even though he or she will be affected by it in a positive way.

For example, let's say someone deceived you. Let's also say you deceived the same person in a past life and you're aware of the karma and the lesson you chose to learn through this experience. You want to clear up the shared karma, but the other person is not ready to balance. You don't have to remain stuck in the relationship or have bad feelings about it. You can balance your part of the karma by being clear about your reasons for wanting to balance, and by resolving your feelings and understanding your reactions about being lied to. This changes your feelings on an inner level about the person and the experience.

As you balance the karma, you see the value of the experience and how it has helped you, and you completely let go of all the negative feelings you have by replacing them with positive feelings, both toward this person and yourself, perhaps using the principle of forgiveness. When you do this, telepathic waves of energy are transmitted to the other person that you've balanced your part of the karma. His or her soul receives and understands the message and feels it on an inner spiritual level.

You're no longer tied to this person because you've experienced and balanced the karma you needed to experience with him or her. The balancing is mirrored in your life by what you've learned from the experience, and in the way you feel about the person and the situation now. The balancing is enhanced and improved upon by the positive way you apply the lesson you've learned to all the aspects of your life. The balancing is manifested in the experiences you have with people who are honest and truthful with you.

When your partner in the shared karma chooses to balance, he or she will create the appropriate circumstances that will enable them to balance. He will find someone with a similar need to have the experience, or will place himself in a situation that will offer the opportunity to balance. The scenarios in the situation or relationship that he sets up will be determined by what he needs to experience to obtain understanding and achieve balance. He may have already learned his lesson by seeing how you responded to the situation; or he may need to experience being deceived in order to know what it's like and to resolve his feelings about it; or he may create a situation where a deception becomes tempting, but he won't engage in it, preferring to learn honesty instead.

You may find yourself drawn back into a relationship with this individual when he or she is ready to balance. If this occurs, it's due to one of two reasons. Although you've already balanced your karma with this person, you choose to help the person by being the catalyst through which the other person balances. If he or she tries to deceive you again, it could be a test to determine if you've completed the balancing and learned the lesson by how you respond to the situation.

Sometimes, with shared karma, you can balance only part of it, or you may choose to delay the balancing until later in this life. To take the above example a step further, let's say the deception was very serious and led to extreme feelings of negativity. At that time, you chose not to resolve your feelings for any number of reasons. Now, several years later, you want to balance the karma, but you can't quite bring yourself to completely let go of all the negativity, even though you'd like to. You'd rather not involve yourself in a relationship with the person again, or perhaps the person is no longer living. You can balance what you feel ready to balance, and clear up a major portion of your karma by understanding and resolving some of your past and present feelings toward this person and the experience.

The unfinished karma will be carried forward into a future lifetime, and will tie you to experiencing some type of situation or relationship with this person. What you experience in a future lifetime with the other person will be determined by why the situation originally occurred in a past life, how it was perpetuated in this lifetime, and by what you wanted to learn from the experience. Only by completely resolving the negativity are you free of the experience. The positive steps you've taken in the present to resolve and understand the negativity will also be carried forward, and the future situation will reflect what you've learned and balanced in this lifetime.

THE TEST OF BALANCING

After you've balanced your karma, you'll be tested to determine if you've learned the lesson beyond any possibility of relapse or failure. You'll find yourself in a similar or related situation to see whether you've really balanced the karma, or whether the balancing was only on a beginning level. This test will help you discover whether your karma is balanced, or whether it's hanging in the balance. If you haven't balanced your karma, then instead of being a test, it's the real thing, and you're again being offered the opportunity to balance your karma.

The test can occur at any time after you feel you've balanced your karma. It most often occurs after you've seen the positive changes begin to manifest in your life, though this isn't a hard and fast rule. It usually surfaces as a minor irritation, rather than a major issue. You may not even be aware that the test is related to the balancing. The test almost always comes as a big surprise, and happens when you least expect it.

The test is either a stumbling block or a stepping stone for you. If you worry about the test before it occurs, you'll fail it because you're afraid you'll fail it. You'll get the second version, and more difficult part of the test the next time. If you ignore the situation and hope it'll go away, you'll find that the situation becomes worse. This shows you that you're not yet done with the balancing. If you get hung up with doubts, or fall back into the negativity, you'll create more karma instead of completing it.

If you know you've learned the lesson and balanced your karma, and you treat the situation in a positive way, you'll pass the test with flying colors. The test proves how well you've done and reaffirms the balancing. This test, in one form or another, will recur until the balancing is completed. The test also strengthens whatever area the karma is involved with, and actually helps you to evolve your soul.

HEALING YOUR KARMA
AND MAKING IT ALL BETTER

Once you balance negative karma, it's important to heal both the present and the related past-life event. The reason for healing the event and your emotions is to cleanse and purge any remaining negativity. Cleaning up your act and clearing the energy completes the balancing. By healing the present event, the energies that surround past-life events are changed to reflect your positive feelings. The healing mirrors the balancing in your present life.

In order to balance and heal properly, all the negativity must be brought up to the surface and cleansed by being understood from all aspects, on both a feeling level and an intellectual level. More than likely, this will temporarily bring you down, as the negativity is washed away with the awareness and insight that the healing brings. When you recognize this as part of the cleansing process, you allow the negativity to wash over you without participating in it. Sometimes, this is the test of balancing.

The process of balancing and healing your karma is just like when you cut yourself and incur a wound. The wound needs to be cleansed before it can heal properly. If you ignore it, or cover it up by putting a Band Aid on a dirty wound, it becomes infected, because you've left all the dirt inside. The wound will fester and erupt in negative expressions until it's properly taken care of. When you clean out the wound and remove all the dirt, it will heal perfectly.

There are several ways you can heal past-life events and their corresponding present events. One way is to surround the events of a particular past life and its effects in your present life with white light. This energy will cleanse and purify all the negativity. There are many more ways to heal your karma. You can become aware of the most appropriate way for you by allowing your higher self to show you how, and to help you heal a particular event or an entire lifetime. When the karma is healed, you feel a wonderful and beautiful release.

You'll always receive some type of sign when you've completed the balancing and healed your karma. You can receive confirmation of the balancing in your dreams, or in a meditation by seeing an image that symbolizes the healing. Most often, it comes through in your awareness of what you've balanced, and by seeing the positive changes mirrored in your present life. You'll feel it in and through your soul, and it will be reflected in your attitude, your actions, and your experiences.

Balancing bad karma creates good karma. That's the beauty of balancing. In addition to all the positive benefits you receive by completely balancing your karma, you'll also find many fringe benefits. As you balance one event, it influences and affects other related events and emotions. You may discover that several other situations become balanced simultaneously without any extra effort. This is because of the positive energy you radiate in your life. The best fringe benefit of balancing is that it brings you happiness, inner peace, and harmony. You gain knowledge and spiritual wisdom, and you evolve your soul.

Opening-Up Exercises

As you understand and balance negative karma that was incurred in previous lives, you can bring up unresolved emotions. It is imperative to use the white-light protection when you begin to look into both the past and the present to understand your karma. In the process of balancing your karma, it's always best to go through your higher self for insight and answers. Your higher self can explain everything you experience and the reasons for your karma. Your higher self will guide you through understanding, balancing, and healing your karma, as well as helping you to move forward in your life and to acquire spiritual knowledge through your experiences.

At all times while balancing your karma, you must be true to your feelings. You might want to go into your inner sanctuary to be in touch with how you really feel about the karma you want to balance. This will help you uncover emotional blockages, or show you any inner reluctance you need to remove before you're ready to balance.

If you're not ready to balance, there's always a good reason for it. You may need to experience the karma in more depth in order to understand it better, or you may only need to reframe your feelings and your perceptions. Work with your feelings in the way that is most appropriate for you. Allow your feelings to help you balance.

If you know—inside—that you're really ready to balance, then allow your higher self to guide you and show you the best and most positive way for you to balance your karma. Listen to your inner voice and follow your feelings. Draw upon your own powerful inner resources and trust yourself. Balance your karma in the way that feels most right for you by doing what your inner guidance tells you to do.

In your journal, keep an ongoing record of the karma you're balancing. Write down what the karma is and why you're balancing it. This helps you see your underlying reasons, and helps you understand your motives. Write down all the images you become aware of in any meditations you engage in. The images and symbols will reveal many aspects of your karma and your current feelings about it. If you take action to balance shared karma, note the other person's reactions to what you do. Write down all your thoughts, feelings, actions, and reactions to events that occur before, during, and after the balancing.

When the karma is balanced, complete and perfect it by doing a healing on it. Write down how you healed it, and how you felt when it was perfectly healed. When the process of balancing is complete, write down all the benefits you've achieved and everything you've learned from the experience. This will show you how the universal Law of Balance is manifested in your life, as well as showing you how you're evolving and perfecting your soul.

PART IV

ENLIGHTENMENT

18

Discovering Your Destiny

Since time began, people have asked the question, "Why am I here and what am I meant to do with my life?" They've wondered and wandered and searched for the answer, trying to solve the mystery of life and looking for the meaning of their own lives. They've traveled through their experiences in the pursuit of their purpose, gaining knowledge with every step. The more they looked for answers, the more they awakened their awareness and found that true answers were within themselves, waiting only for their recognition. When recognized, they revealed the truth. When accepted, they opened up higher horizons of awareness and knowledge. The path you follow to find your purpose leads you on a true course toward your destiny and the fulfillment of goals you've chosen to accomplish in this lifetime.

Your destiny and your dharma are why you chose physical existence. Destiny encompasses the lessons you chose to learn and the karma you chose to balance. *Dharma* is the main purpose your soul strives for in every lifetime. Discovering your destiny and finding your dharma is like watching a rose open up, petal by petal. As you travel through the journey of life, your destiny unfolds step by step, revealing your dharma within your experiences.

As you pursue your dharma, you understand why you're here. As you attain your dharma, you discover the meaning in your life and you understand your purpose. As you express your dharma, you reach your soul's purpose, and you become aware that it's a gift you share, both with yourself and with others. Through your destiny, you evolve your soul and gain knowledge. Through your dharma, you acquire spiritual wisdom and attain levels of enlightenment.

Dharma differs from lifetime to lifetime, depending on what your soul chooses to experience and perfect. You chose the path to follow in this life that would enable you to reach your destiny. You created the events and experiences that would allow you to accomplish your purpose. Your dharma is determined, in part, from your soul's purpose in previous lives, and from your actions and reactions to the events and experiences that occurred. Your destiny may be a continuation of previous goals, and of working through karma you've incurred that interfered with your purpose in past lives. Your dharma is directed by the wisdom of your soul in creating your current experiences, and by the choices and decisions you make in this lifetime.

While your dharma may relate to or involve karma you need to balance, it's usually a culmination of efforts and achievements. Your dharma may be one central purpose that is woven together with other achievements, and can range anywhere from being a good person to learning a lesson to achieving something or to saving the world. Dharma doesn't have to be an idealistic, or noble, or even a spiritual purpose. It can be something that is physically oriented. The value of dharma begins with how you feel about yourself and what you want to accomplish. Your dharma is special to you and evolves your soul by allowing you to experience and develop higher aspects of yourself.

No matter what path you take, all roads lead you toward your destiny. You can discover the path you chose to follow to reach your dharma in two different ways. Some people insist on doing things the hard way and going against their destiny, rather than going with the flow. If you choose to travel a rocky route, then you have to see through the maze of mystery that clouds your destiny to find out where your life is leading you. Look at the way your life is going and how you feel about the goals in your life. Look at your reasons for wanting them, your motives for achieving them, and how you feel when you reach your goals.

If you have to fight for everything you want, and if everything you want has been determined or directed by other people, you're not closely tuned into your spiritual nature, and you're not following the path that connects you with your destiny and your dharma. If you find that you're achieving unhappiness and despair instead of happiness and fulfillment, then you're pursuing a purpose that goes against your destiny.

Every choice you've made in the past, and every choice you make in the present, affects and alters your destiny, leading you closer to your dharma with every twist and turn of fate. If you're following a path that is contrary to what your soul desires to accomplish, you'll experience problems that will escalate and become more serious until you get back on the right path. At first, you might mistake this as karma, but if you look closely, you'll see that you're stuck in a negative pattern and following the wrong path.

Events in your life that appear to be out of your control show you how you're honoring commitments and covenants you made before your birth. When you realize why these events are happening, and you recognize your feelings about them, you'll see the wisdom within your experiences by how they guide you toward the path you've chosen to follow. When you change direction, through the course of your experiences, you'll find the way back to your path.

Discovering your destiny is finding the right path to follow. To know if your path is right for you, listen to your feelings and trust your inner knowledge. You intuitively know the direction of your destiny by following your feelings that guide you to your truth.

When you're on the path that's right for you, you sense it and you feel it on a deep, spiritual level within yourself. You know that what you want to achieve and what you're doing is the right thing for you, no matter what anyone else says or thinks. You're guided by an innate sense of direction and by your spiritual wisdom.

If you choose to travel a clear and shining path, you can discover your dharma by noticing what comes to you easily and by what you enjoy doing. When you're following the direction of your destiny, the things you want or need seem to flow to you without any effort. While these things are often the rewards of past-life achievements, they're also a good indication of the path you chose to help you achieve your dharma. When you go with the flow of your destiny, you experience a natural awareness of your purpose.

The difference between dharma and past-life rewards are how you feel about them in the present and the importance you place on them. Past achievements bring you pleasure and happiness, and you enjoy them. Dharma may be something that builds upon your past-life achievements and your present accomplishments, but it's more of a respect for and dedication to your purpose that leads you forward. Dharma is an experience of searching for and finding the treasures of your soul. It's a joyful and completely fulfilling pursuit of what you want to accomplish.

Finding your dharma is finding your niche in the world. When you're pursuing your purpose, you're tuned into your spiritual nature and you're in harmony with it. In the process, you learn about yourself and you grow spiritually. Dharma is always something positive, even if you have to struggle or work hard to achieve it. You feel an inner satisfaction when you're directing your efforts toward reaching your dharma. You enjoy what you're doing in every moment, and it brings you happiness and fulfillment on every level. When you achieve your dharma, you evolve into higher levels of awareness and enlightenment.

Opening-Up Exercises

Exercise 1. The answer to what your purpose is can be found in the present. Your dharma is either what you're doing now with your life or what you want to do with it. What you've already accomplished may be a stepping stone to your dharma. Your experiences, your feelings, your interests, and your work or career all point to your purpose.

You can discover your dharma by looking at your answers to the Current Clues Questionnaire, specifically the sections on "Career and Job," "Personality Traits and Characteristics," "Friends and Family," and "Interests, Talents, and Hobbies." Your answers will show you what your destiny is and how to achieve your dharma.

Exercise 2. The key issues in your life and their past-life influences that you identified in Chapter 16, "Paying the IOUs From the Past," will show you how you're following the path you've chosen to reach your goals. There are many clues in your life that reveal your destiny and your dharma. The lessons you chose to learn and the karma you chose to balance will give you valuable insights.

If you're dealing with negative issues, look at the positive side of those issues, and you'll have a big clue to part of your purpose. Most important is how you feel about your experiences and the value of them. In learning your lessons, especially the painful ones, perhaps you've already recognized them as being positive experiences that turned your life around and steered you in the direction of your destiny.

Exercise 3. To know what your dharma is in this lifetime, look at what you really want to do and what makes you happy. While the pursuit of happiness is a right granted to you by the laws of the land, it's also a birthright of your spiritual nature. In your journal, make a list of all your hopes, desires, dreams, plans, and goals. Get in touch with your feelings about them, and write down why you want to achieve them and why they're important to you. Notice how some of them are related and build upon one another. This will offer you many insights into yourself and into why you chose the earth experience to fulfill your dharma.

- Notice what you'd like to do more than anything else. If you feel it's unattainable or impossible, then let go of your limits and free yourself to achieve it. Enter an Alpha level and let your thoughts and feelings flow with what you want to do. Allow yourself to experience it and to know what it's like to pursue and achieve what you really want. See yourself achieving it and notice how you feel about it. If you're already doing what you want, then expand on it. In your journal, write down what you experienced in your reverie. Your desires will reflect your dharma, and you may be closer to achieving it than you think.

- If you feel it's really unattainable in this lifetime, then look at the experiences in your life that relate to what you want to do and help to form it. In your journal, note the events that lead up to, or are similar to, what you want to do, and connect them with your desires. The way your experiences relate to what you really want to accomplish, and how you feel about them, will give you clues to what your dharma is.

  You may be forming the foundation for your dharma in a future life, or you may be only a step away from recognizing it. You may need to look at it from a different perspective in order to see it clearly. The similarities in your experiences will show you what your dharma is, and the connections will provide you with the awareness that you may have already begun to accomplish your dharma.

- If you feel it's just out of your reach, then refer to your list from #3 as a background and write down the things that flow naturally into your life. Include the experiences you have that follow the direction of your hopes, desires, dreams, plans, and goals. Note the events and experiences that make you feel like you're on the right path and the ones that lead you toward what you want to accomplish. Note the situations that make you feel happy, comfortable, and natural, and the ones that bring you fulfillment.

  This list will expand upon your previous lists and will show you that you already have the awareness of your purpose. Notice how some of your experiences have influenced and affected other experiences. Notice how your emotions have formed your decisions. This list will reveal the steps you've taken on your path and the things you've already accomplished that have led you closer to achieving your purpose.

Exercise 4. You may have several purposes to accomplish in this lifetime, but there is generally one very specific goal or one very high attainment of your soul's desire. Look over your previous lists and answers. As you go through your notes, you may discover that several items surfaced on every list and became more clearly defined as you added more information and became aware of more insights.

In your journal, write down eleven goals that are very important to you. Your goals can be hopes, desires, dreams, plans, or wishes. Include the ones you value most, the ones in progress, the ones you've already accomplished, and the ones you feel special about. These goals can be physical, mental, emotional, or spiritual. They can show experiences, lessons, karma, or the things you'd like to improve on. They can reflect your innermost thoughts and feelings.

- From this list, choose seven goals that you feel are your dharma in this life. In your journal, write down why you feel destined to achieve them and what motivates you. Note all the steps you've already taken toward achieving them. This will give you even more information as it reveals important clues and insights into your destiny and your dharma.

- Look at your list of seven items very carefully and thoughtfully. Circle the one goal you feel most drawn to accomplish. The goal you've circled is your primary soul goal— your dharma. The other six are your secondary soul goals—your destiny. They show you the particular lessons you chose to learn and the karma you chose to balance that are most important in helping you to gain knowledge and evolve on those levels. The other items from your list show past-life rewards and what you came back to enjoy on a physical level.

YOU ARE THE MASTER OF YOUR FATE

You're in control of your life and your destiny. Every event you encounter has been chosen and created by you. Your present life has been formed by your thoughts, shaped by your feelings, and molded from the events and emotions in your past lives. Every experience you've ever had, and every emotion you've ever felt, have led you closer to reaching the perfection of your soul.

You've allowed yourself to become all that you are through the process of evolving your soul during your physical incarnations. When you look at where you are now, perhaps in relation to where you want to be in the future, and where you've been in the past, you find that the perfect place to be is in the present. The present is your foothold into the future and your foundation from the past. As you live every moment of every lifetime in the present, being true to who you are and how you feel, you're respecting your spirituality and you're honoring your life. You're embracing who you've been before, who you are now, and who you will become. Living in the here and now, in all of your past, present, and future lives, is timeless.

Your destiny is right here, right now, in the present. You're where you want to be, and where you're meant to be, at all times in your life, even if you feel lost or you're not sure of your next step. Maybe all you have to do is look in front of you to see your way. Maybe you've just begun your search to find your path. The search itself could be the direction that leads you to your dharma. In trying to understand the reason for your life, you discover your purpose. In striving to achieve your dharma, you fulfill your destiny.

Maybe you're already on your path toward your dharma and you're watching your destiny unfold, step by step, just like a rose opens up, petal by petal, in accordance with its own timing, revealing itself in a natural manner. Maybe you've reached your dharma, and you only have to recognize it and accept it. Maybe you've found your dharma and the rose is completely open, showing a very beautiful flower in full bloom.

Opening-Up Exercises

Exercise 1. Understanding why you chose your dharma, and discovering the direction of your path that has led you through your destiny into reaching your dharma, will answer the question of why you're here and what you're meant to be doing with your life this time. You're the only one who can answer this question. Look within yourself and you'll find the truth.

Enter an Alpha level and allow your higher self to guide you into and through a meditation that will open up your knowledge and show you the truth within yourself. Focus on an image of a rose and watch the rose as it opens up, petal by petal, revealing the knowledge within its center. Project yourself into the rose as it opens up. Allow yourself to become the rose and feel yourself opening up the knowledge and truth within yourself. Watch how your awareness unfolds, step by step, as the rose opens up, petal by petal.

A rose is an occult [hidden] symbol of inner knowledge and truth, opening up and responding to your desire for the truth and knowledge that is within yourself. In your journal, write down everything you experienced and became aware of as you opened up your knowledge and found the truth within yourself.

Exercise 2. In the following meditations, allow your higher self to guide you as you explore the paths you've traveled in the past and the present, and the path you'll travel in the future that will lead you to fulfilling your dharma. These meditations blend into one another and show you the direction of your destiny in a free-flowing manner that enables you to discover why you chose your dharma. After each meditation, write down everything you experience, explore, and become aware of. Include what your higher self shows you, what your higher self tells you, and where your higher self leads you.

- Look into your past lives to see why you've chosen your dharma. Let your mind flow through the purposes you're pursuing in this lifetime. Allow images of the past-life origins of your present dharma to surface, and become aware of the past-life influences that affect your current destiny. Feel the experiences and the emotions that show you why you chose your dharma, and how they've formed the path you follow now to find your purpose. Notice how the path you've followed in the past has led you to your present path. As you become aware of the past-life events and emotions that have formed the steps on your path, and you connect them with your present experiences, you'll find the answer to the question of why you're here.

- Look at where you are in your life right now. Backtrack through your past in this lifetime to see the path you've traveled that has led you toward your purpose. As you look at the direction your path has followed, you'll notice that your choices, decisions, and even seemingly unrelated events are woven into the path that leads you toward reaching your dharma. As you look at the direction you've followed to arrive at your destiny, and you see how all the steps you've taken in the present have formed your path toward your dharma, you'll find the answer to the question of what you're meant to be doing with your life this time.

- Look into the future and see the steps in front of you that have been formed from your steps in your past lives and in your present life. Notice how each step has led from one experience to another, and how all the steps ultimately lead you to fulfilling your soul's purpose in this lifetime. As you look at the direction you've traveled from the past into the present, you'll see all the steps before you that are waiting for you to travel them, and you'll discover how to achieve your dharma. As you look at where you've been, where you are now, and where you're going, you'll find the answer to the question of why your soul chose to reincarnate and the reasons why you've followed the path that you have.

- Look beyond the physical expression of your dharma to see the true purpose within your dharma. As you find the spiritual meaning of your dharma, you'll discover what your soul desires to accomplish. As you understand how your soul expresses itself through dharma, you'll see how you acquire spiritual wisdom and attain higher levels of enlightenment.

- Look beyond the physical nature of the past, present, and future steps you've seen in your meditations and discover the path of knowledge that leads you to your soul and to higher horizons of evolvement. This is a timeless path of spirituality that your soul travels, leading to awareness and enlightenment. Allow your higher self to guide you as you walk the path. Every step you take will give you answers to questions you haven't asked yet and answers to questions you weren't aware of before.

Look through all the notes you've written and all the insights you've become aware of in these meditations. When you put them all together, you'll be looking at a complete picture of your destiny and your dharma in this lifetime. You'll see how it was formed, why you chose it, and where you're going with it. The information you've gained will show you that you are the master of your fate. The knowledge you've become aware of will show you how your soul expresses itself and how you're evolving your soul. You'll discover the treasures within your soul as you look within yourself and find your truth.

19

The Energy Essence of YOU

Desire for truth and knowledge is the first step on your path toward wisdom and enlightenment. As you discover your truth and become aware of your knowledge within, you begin to follow your path that leads you to understanding your true spiritual nature. As you continue upon your path, you increase your spiritual wisdom with the light of understanding, and you recognize your soul as the immortal, eternal energy that is you.

As you begin to understand your spiritual nature, you begin to understand how the energy of your soul expresses and manifests itself in your physical incarnation. As you recognize the energies of your soul, you understand yourself and your experiences. You see how they're formulated, created, manifested, and expressed in the various levels of physical and spiritual energy.

Energy is, was, and always will be. Everything is composed of energy vibrations, manifesting in various forms and expressions. You are spiritual energy embodied in physical form. Within the energy essence of you are layers and levels of energy and awareness. Your inner self is the energy vibration of beliefs and feelings.

Your higher self is the energy vibration of truth and knowledge. Your soul is a pure energy vibration of awareness and enlightenment, expressing itself in and through the energies of your inner self and your higher self and manifesting itself through your experiences.

Each vibration of energy has its own unique properties and qualities. As you change your level of energy vibration, you become aware of and in tune with that particular vibration of energy, and you understand its properties and qualities. Raising your level of awareness above physical energies enables you to tune into higher levels of energy and to open up your inner truth and knowledge. As you move upward into and through the higher vibrations of spiritual energy, you obtain a true understanding of your soul and the nature of your experiences.

YOUR PYRAMID OF POWER

You express yourself through your own unique and individual nature, and you experience a different level of awareness in each vibration of energy. Each level of energy forms the foundation and framework for higher levels of awareness. Since you are spiritual energy, you have the power to influence, affect, and change energy. Your beliefs form the basis of how you influence and affect the energy that creates your experiences. You channel, change, and direct energy through your feelings and thoughts. Your beliefs, thoughts, and feelings determine everything you experience and how the energy manifests in your life. Your perceptions of your experiences form your physical reality and create the framework of your spiritual awareness.

Your feelings are formed by your beliefs, and are manifested in the expression of your experiences. Your thoughts are created from your feelings and by your experiences, and are transformed into truth and knowledge. Your truth and knowledge is manifested in your understanding of your experiences, and is transformed into wisdom and enlightenment. As you understand your feelings, thoughts, and experiences, you acquire awareness. Within your awareness, you discover the essence of your soul and you understand your spiritual nature.

Energy pyramids and builds upon itself, growing and expanding into power. Since you are energy, you also pyramid yourself through the energies of your inner self, your higher self, and your soul. You begin with your inner self by being in touch with your feelings. As you become in touch with your feelings and understand your responses to your experiences, you become aware of your inner truth. As you accept your inner truth, your knowledge increases and you acquire awareness.

As you continue to raise your energy vibration to a higher level of awareness, you become in tune with your higher self. Through the energy vibration of your higher self and your increased awareness, you build the power to acquire spiritual knowledge through your experiences, which expands into the awareness of your soul. Your awareness is then filtered through your feelings, thoughts, and knowledge, and is understood on every level of energy.

As your awareness continues to grow and expand, you experience the energies as a natural and flowing process that spirals upward through higher echelons of awareness, in rhythm and harmony with understanding. As you raise your level of awareness to understand the energy vibration of your soul, you acquire spiritual awareness. This awareness enables you to see through the physical aspects and expressions of your feelings, thoughts, and experiences with the complete wisdom of understanding, which is enlightenment. This forms your pyramid of power.

The energy vibrations of your inner self, your higher self, and your soul are steps to truth, leading upward to enlightenment. These steps form the foundation and provide the structure and framework for you to acquire knowledge and to raise your awareness to higher levels during your physical incarnation. These steps of awareness are in harmony with an even higher level of energy that blends your knowledge into a unity of understanding.

LAYERS AND LEVELS OF ENERGY AND AWARENESS

The energies and expressions of your inner self, your higher self, and your soul are layered in levels of energy and awareness within you. Each of these seven layers is known as a *chakra*, which is an energy spiral vibrating on a certain frequency, corresponding with a particular level of awareness. Each chakra expresses its unique nature and qualities in different levels of awareness, and governs what you experience in each vibration of energy. Within the vibrations of the many aspects of yourself and your experiences is a world of knowledge and awareness.

The energy layers of your chakras are represented by the energies of the seven colors of the rainbow. To oversimplify their expressions, and what you experience in each level of awareness, look at the rainbow as waves of energy, vibrating to higher levels of awareness within each color. As you progress upward through the colors, your awareness increases in each vibration as the energies blend and flow into one another and expand.

The rainbow begins with the color red, which vibrates to physical energies and forms your perception of your reality. The rainbow flows into the color orange, which vibrates to emotional energies. Together, they form the essence of your feelings and your physical reality, and your level of energy and awareness within your inner self.

The rainbow continues with the color yellow, which vibrates to mental energies and thoughts, and is the beginning level of your inner knowledge. The rainbow expands into the color green, which vibrates to spiritual energies and growth, and is a higher expression of your feelings. This is the center point between physical and spiritual energies. Blue vibrates to astral energies, and is your knowledge in motion. Indigo vibrates to etheric energies, and is your awareness in a higher spiritual framework of wisdom and understanding. These colors form the essence of knowledge and the energy and awareness of your higher self.

The color violet at the top of the rainbow vibrates to the energies of your soul, and forms your spiritual awareness. All together, the vibrations and expressions of the colors of the rainbow form the energy essence of you. The white mist above the rainbow vibrates to universal energies, and forms your enlightenment. These are the same energies you travel, in reverse, as you reincarnate into a new physical body.

The energy of your soul flows within and through every level of your awareness during your present incarnation. Your soul assumes a physical expression of energy within the vibrations of your inner self and your higher self, and manifests itself in and through your experiences. The energies of your soul participate in and transcend the physical energies that surround you during your present incarnation. Through your physical and spiritual awareness, you absorb and filter knowledge in your own unique manner of understanding, and you express your awareness in your experiences. As you increase your understanding of your experiences and your knowledge, you evolve into even higher levels and vibrations of energy and awareness.

Opening-Up Exercises

The energy essence of you, in order to be completely understood, must be experienced. Words can explain the basic principles, but understanding requires the knowledge of experience. You've felt this energy many times before when you've entered an Alpha level, and when you've influenced your energy vibrations through your feelings and thoughts. You've experienced the flow of energy every time you've raised your energies to a higher level of awareness. You've felt the vibrations of energy change when you've traveled the colors of the rainbow.

Layers of Energy

Enter an Alpha level and feel the difference in your level of awareness within each color of the rainbow. Notice what you experience within each energy vibration of the colors. This will help you understand what each of your chakras influences and governs. Be very aware of the change in the vibrations of energy, and feel the rhythm in the flow of energy as you raise your level of awareness. (You might also want to review the rainbow visualization in Chapter 3 "Meeting Your Subconscious Mind.")

As you begin to absorb the energies of red and orange, and you begin to enter an Alpha level, notice how relaxed your body is, and

*how aware your mind is. As you become in tune with the energies
of your inner self and your feelings, you can feel the rhythm in the
flow of energy as you begin to feel and absorb the energies of the
color yellow. As you raise your level of awareness to feel and
experience higher vibrations of energy, notice how much more
relaxed your body is, and how much more aware your mind is.*

*As you absorb the energies of the color green in the rainbow,
center your awareness into the energies of your higher self. As you
feel the vibrations of higher levels of energy, you become in tune
with the energies of your spiritual knowledge and the color blue.
Feel the gradual rhythm in the flow of energy as you continue to
raise your awareness into even higher vibrations of energy, and
you absorb the color indigo. As you rise through the energies of
the rainbow and you increase your level of awareness, you enter
and absorb the energies of the color violet as you expand into the
energies of your soul.*

In your journal, write down what you experienced in each
individual level of awareness and energy in the colors of the
rainbow. This will help you understand the energies within you,
and how the energy is expressed through you and your experiences.
Write down how you felt as you increased your awareness of your
energy vibrations, and how you experienced the flow of awareness
between the energy vibrations of each color. This will help you
understand how your soul transcends physical energies and travels
through spiritual energies.

Levels of Awareness

Your energy essence begins within your feelings, and radiates and
expands through higher levels of energy. As you center into the
energies of your inner self and your feelings, and you raise your
awareness, you become in tune with the energies of your higher self
and your knowledge. As you acquire and accept your knowledge,
you tune into even higher levels of awareness and spiritual vibrations of energy, and you become aware of the energies of your soul
and your spiritual essence.

The following candle meditation will help you raise your awareness above physical energies by centering your attention on the higher aspects of energy within yourself. Focusing on higher levels of awareness will put you more in touch with the spiritual energies and expressions of your inner self and your higher self, and will help you tune into the energy vibrations of your soul and your true spiritual nature. The center of the flame represents your inner self. The flame of the candle represents your higher self. The aura, which is the energy essence of the flame, represents your soul. Before you begin, light a white candle and enter an Alpha level.

Look into the center of the flame of the candle. Focus your attention and your awareness into and around the flame of the candle. As you focus your thoughts on the flame and you sense its energy, you center in on your self-awareness, and you begin to become aware of the energies within you.

Look into the center of the flame. Feel the energy within you as you enter a more aware level of mind. Feel yourself expanding into a higher level of awareness as you become in tune with the energies of your feelings. As you continue to look into the center of the flame, you begin to feel the energy vibrations of your inner self. You begin to focus into the energies of your feelings as you continue to raise your energy vibrations to a more aware level.

Sense the energy that emanates from within the center of the flame. Become aware of the positive energy that emanates from within you. Feel the energy that radiates from within the center of your awareness. Allow the energies of your inner self and your feelings to expand and flow into a higher level of awareness. Become more and more aware of your energy source within, and feel the energy as it begins to expand inside of you.

As you become more aware of the energy of your inner self, you become more in touch with your feelings. You feel completely in tune with your inner self, and you're perfectly aware of your energy source within. You're more aware of your true feelings, which lead you to the truth and knowledge you have within yourself.

In your own way, and in the manner that is most appropriate for you, be in touch with your natural awareness of your inner self. Become more in tune with the vibrations of your inner self, and become more aware of your inner feelings. Go within the center of your awareness, and feel the energy vibrations that form the beginning of your spiritual essence. Become aware of the light and life within you that begins inside your soul and radiates and expands all around you.

*   *   *   *

Look at the flame of the candle. Focus your attention and your awareness into the entire flame of the candle. Become aware of the energy that emanates from the flame. Begin to raise your energies to a higher level of awareness. Feel yourself attaining a more aware level of mind. As you look at the flame of the candle and you sense its energy, you begin to feel the energies of your truth and knowledge opening up inside of you and expanding into even higher levels of energy and awareness.

Focus on the energy within you and begin to feel the energy vibrations of your inner truth and knowledge. Begin to feel the energy vibrations of your higher self. Become more aware of the positive energy that emanates from within you and radiates through your inner truth and knowledge. Feel the energy that emanates from a higher vibration of truth and knowledge within you. Feel the energy vibration of your higher self and become more and more aware of the energy that emanates and radiates from your higher self. As you become more in tune with your higher levels of energy and awareness, you expand into the full awareness of your higher self.

Feel the increase in the energy vibrations of knowledge within you. Center into your source of knowledge and truth within to reach even higher levels of energy and awareness. Focus into the higher vibrations of the energy of your truth and knowledge. As you feel the energy of your higher truth and knowledge, you become aware of the increased energy that emanates from your higher self and flows from your source of knowledge and truth within.

As you become aware of your higher source of energy, you become more aware of your spiritual knowledge. You become more aware of the truth and knowledge you have within yourself, and you recognize the true awareness of your experiences and knowledge. You completely understand your feelings about your experiences. As you understand your feelings, you become more aware of the truth within your knowledge.

In your own way, and in the manner that is most appropriate for you, become more aware of the energy vibrations of your higher self. Become more aware of the truth and knowledge you have within you. Become more and more in tune with the awareness of your higher self, and feel the energy that emanates and radiates from your higher self and expands into the awareness of your soul.

* * * * *

Look around the flame of the candle at the aura of energy around the flame. The aura is the energy essence of the flame. The aura begins within and radiates from its center, just as the energy and expression of your soul begins within and radiates from the center of your feelings, flows into your knowledge, and then expands into your spirituality, forming your energy essence.

Focus your awareness into the energy of the flame's aura. Center your awareness into the energy essence of you. Become aware of the pure and positive energy that emanates from within you, and radiates and expands all around you. Begin to feel the energy that emanates from your soul. Feel the pure and positive vibrations that emanate from within you and radiate through your energy essence.

Focus your awareness within your energy essence. Become aware of the energy vibrations of your soul. As you become aware of your energy essence that begins within and expands and radiates all around you, you feel a warm, flowing movement begin to vibrate inside of you. It feels like the pulsing of a heartbeat, spreading energy and awareness within you and all around you.

As you feel your energy essence within you and all around you, you become more and more aware that you are a spiritual being. You become more aware of your spiritual energies that transcend physical energies. Completely immerse yourself in the pure energy vibration of your soul. Feel it expanding inside of you, and radiating from within the center of yourself.

As you look at the energy and light that emanates and radiates from the flame of the candle, you become aware of the light and energy that begins within your soul, and emanates and radiates from within the center of your awareness. You become aware that you are the energy of light, and you become aware of the true essence of your soul. As you become more and more aware of your soul, the flame becomes brighter and brighter.

In your own way, and in the manner that is most appropriate for you, become more aware of your soul and your energy essence. Become more in tune with the pure energy vibration of your soul. Allow yourself to become more and more aware of your true spiritual nature. Visualize, sense, and feel your energy essence. Close your eyes and meditate, being very aware of the energy vibration of your soul.

* * * * *

When you're done with your meditation, take a deep breath. As you breathe in, allow yourself to absorb all the knowledge you've become aware of. Bring inside of you the complete awareness and understanding of your soul and your energy essence. As you breathe out, filter the knowledge and awareness into your conscious mind, with full understanding of everything you've felt and experienced in your meditation.

In your journal, write down everything you experienced and became aware of. Include what you experienced within the energies of your inner self, your higher self, and your soul. Write down your feelings about your inner self, your awareness of your higher self, and your perceptions of your soul and your energy essence. Note all the images and insights you became aware of during your meditation.

The candle meditation enables you to become more aware of the energies of your inner self, your higher self, and the essence of your soul. Meditating on the flame of the candle helps you attain a more spiritual level of mind by focusing your awareness into the energies within yourself. As you raise your vibrations of energy and your level of awareness, you increase your understanding of your feelings, your experiences, and your knowledge. This offers you the opportunity to expand your awareness even further.

As you become more aware of and in tune with the energy vibrations of your inner self, your higher self, and your soul, you become aware of the true nature of your experiences. As you blend the energies of your feelings, knowledge, and awareness into the complete wisdom of understanding, you become aware of the essence of your soul and your spirituality. As you understand the energies that compose the essence of you, and you unify the energies into a harmony of understanding, you allow yourself to feel, know, and be aware of your soul and the true nature of your spirituality on a higher level of truth. This forms the foundation of your enlightenment.

20

The True Nature of Your Spirituality

Your true nature is that of a free spirit, dressed in the earthly attire of a physical body. Your soul adapts to the physical energies that enable you to exist in a physical environment. Reincarnation is experienced in order to balance karma, learn life lessons, and to accomplish purposes and goals that will advance your soul to higher levels of awareness. In each incarnation, you acquire knowledge that enables you to express your spirituality during your earth experience.

Reincarnation is a step on your path that leads to the perfection of your soul. Through the process of your desire for truth and knowledge, you raise your level of awareness and you rise above the limits and restrictions of physical energies. This awareness enables you to understand how your soul can be free at all times, while temporarily assuming the energies of a physical existence.

As you acquire truth and knowledge through your earth experience, you expand into spiritual and universal energies. As you express your spiritual nature through the physical energies of your experiences, and you raise your level of awareness, you reach a complete understanding of your soul and the reasons for your physical existence. Through this, you acquire spiritual wisdom and attain enlightenment.

Your soul vibrates to spiritual and universal energies, transcending the physical environment by the very nature of itself. Your soul is in tune with the energies of nature and the universe, moving in rhythm with knowledge and awareness, in harmony with light. Your soul has the ability to move through the energies with the ease of understanding. As your soul advances through physical energies, and enters the realm of spiritual and universal energies, your soul becomes free and attains its natural state of existence in its true form.

Within the energies of the universe, you completely understand both your physical nature and your spiritual nature, and you understand the truth about your soul. You understand the earth and the universe, and because you understand them, you know they're both one and the same, with the only difference being in the expression of higher levels of energy. You're aware that the universe above is the same as the earth below, and that knowledge is what enables you to transcend physical energies.

SETTING YOUR SPIRIT FREE

Your soul is the universal energy of light, and you can feel and experience your spirit in its energy form. The following meditation will help you understand your true spiritual nature by allowing you to discover for yourself what you experience within the energy vibration of your soul. By raising your energy vibrations above a physical level, you can become aware of the true nature of your spirituality. Before you begin, enter an Alpha level and go within yourself to your inner sanctuary.

Listen to the sounds of nature and feel at.one with the world within you and around you. Be in touch with your feelings and in tune with your knowledge and your awareness. Breathe in the white-light protection. This will keep you safe on all levels as you explore and experience your soul in its natural form. As you breathe in the white-light protection from universal sources, you begin to feel yourself flowing and floating upward through the energies of yourself.

As you blend your energies into your higher self, you begin to feel open and expansive and free. Allow yourself to flow into the higher energies of knowledge and awareness and light. As you become in tune with your spiritual energies, you begin to feel the essence of your soul. As you allow yourself to experience even higher levels of awareness and knowledge, you feel yourself blending into the magical energies of the universe, in harmony with the earth. As you harmonize and raise your energies into a unity of spiritual and universal energies, you begin to understand your soul and the true nature of your spirituality.

In your inner sanctuary, you notice a beautiful butterfly sitting on the leaf of a tree. The butterfly has very delicate and unusual colorings and markings. It's almost as if the butterfly is transparent. The butterfly has just emerged into the light, and is just beginning to expand its wings to fly. As it opens its wings, you see them shimmering in the sunlight. You can see the golden chrysalis nearby, where the butterfly emerged from.

Your soul is like a butterfly that's free. As you unwrap the physical cocoon of energies, and you break through the paperlike shell of limited consciousness, you open up the veil of awareness and you set your spirit free. As you loosen the blinds of restriction through your awareness, you transcend physical energies, moving upward into the light of your soul and your spiritual energies. As you continue to rise even higher into universal energies, your soul becomes open and free.

Being in tune with nature, you're in harmony with yourself and with everything around you. You understand what the butterfly feels like as it begins to fly and soar ... as it frees itself and floats on natural currents of air, enjoying the light and sunshine all around it ... rising and soaring through the clouds. You almost feel like you could rise and soar with the butterfly, in harmony with air and light. You almost feel like you could rise and soar into

*the universe, being free of physical boundaries and limits . . .
moving upward through the clouds toward the light.*

*You almost feel as if you're the butterfly. As you become in tune
with the energies of the butterfly, you understand its natural
harmony with the energies of the earth and the universe. You
become aware of your natural harmony with spiritual energies. As
you become in tune with the energies of your spiritual nature, you
become aware that you can transcend earthly energies and flow
into universal energies of awareness and light.*

*As the butterfly begins to float and fly and soar, you feel
yourself floating upward, emerging and expanding into knowledge
and light. The butterfly is free . . . flying, soaring, floating above
the earth . . . and you feel just as free. You're free of the clouds of
physical energies, and you've emerged into the energy of your
spirit. You feel your spirit begin to fly and soar and expand into
knowledge and awareness and light.*

*As you fly and soar upward, higher and higher, you can feel the
freedom of knowledge and the warmth of awareness. As you feel
the light from the sunshine and you float on natural currents of
air, you feel yourself becoming more and more free. You can see
sparkles of light and energy that look like glistening jewels that
illuminate the sky. The sparkles of light look like stars and rays of
sunshine, and they feel warm and peaceful and nourishing as they
shower you with awareness. As you absorb the light and energy of
the universe, you feel the energy within you and around you. You
feel illuminated with the natural energy and light of sunshine. You
feel the vibrations of universal energies, and you're in harmony
with the universe.*

*You fly and soar upward into the universe, higher and higher,
becoming more and more free . . . transcending the earthly pull of
physical energies . . . expanding into ever-widening horizons of
true knowledge and awareness . . . flying on wings of illumination
and light . . . as you explore and experience your soul in its natural
form. Your spirit is free . . . flying and soaring and expanding into
the universe. You move with the motion and rhythm of knowledge*

*and awareness and light. You experience the universe in harmony
with yourself. You're filled with light and you are light.*

*   *   *   *   *

*And now it's time to come back down to earth. Feel yourself
gradually descending through the energies of the universe and
entering the energies of the earth. Feel yourself gently lighting
upon a leaf of a tree, absorbing all the knowledge you've become
aware of; feeling very peaceful and nourished from the universe
and from within yourself.*

In your journal, write down everything you experienced and
became aware of as you set your spirit free and explored your true
spiritual nature. Write down your awareness and understanding of
your spirituality. Include your awareness of universal energies, and
how the universe operates in harmony with the earth. This will
help you understand the process and purpose of reincarnation and
the reasons for rebirth. It will help you know and understand why
your soul chooses a physical expression of its energies, and why the
earth experience is one of the steps on your journey home.

21

The Puzzle Pieces of Your Past Lives

Your past lives are a treasure chest of knowledge and truth that is filled with insight and awareness into yourself, and into the events and emotions you experience in your present life. As you balance your karma, learn your life lessons, and pursue your dharma, the puzzle pieces begin to fit together perfectly. Your beliefs, thoughts, feelings, and experiences show you your truth and reveal an intimate portrait of your soul. Your past lives and your present life show you how you express your soul, and how you acquire truth and knowledge as you evolve spiritually into higher levels of awareness and enlightenment.

The opening-up exercises and meditations given in this book contain the instructions for assembling and connecting all the clues. Your journal provides you with all the pieces of the puzzle, and gives you the key to understanding your past lives as it opens up your treasure chest of truth and knowledge. As you put the clues together, you solve the mystery of what happened in your past lives and you find out who did what to whom.

As you put the pieces of the puzzle together, you see a clear picture that shows you how your current experiences are directly related to your past-life experiences through the Law of Karma. As the puzzle comes together, it offers you the answers to why you're experiencing your present life and gives you the awareness of your spiritual evolvement.

If there are any missing pieces of your memories, you can find them and fill in the blanks by reexperiencing those parts of your past lives in the way that is most appropriate for you. Allow your higher self to guide you as you see and feel your past-life experiences. Watch the emotions and events as they portray themselves in your mind, and allow your past lives to tell you everything you want to know. Draw in the connections and correlations to your present life. Add your insights and perceptions and put the pieces of the puzzle together with your understanding. Notice how the past and the present fit together perfectly and interlock once they're connected.

With the understanding and knowledge you've acquired on your journey through your past lives, you might want to look through some of the earlier entries in your journal that provided you with opening keys and clues. Tie up any loose ends by redoing some of the opening-up exercises and meditations you feel are important. As you go more in-depth with your answers and your experiences, you'll find even more valuable insights into understanding your past lives.

All the puzzle pieces of your past lives form a very beautiful picture of your soul. When the clues are connected and the puzzle is put together, the picture shows you how all of the events and emotions in your past lives have influenced and shaped your present life. As you look at the completed puzzle, you become aware of how your present life will influence and affect your future lives and your spiritual evolvement. Within your present life, through the positive use of your free will, you can create a picture that is a masterpiece.

22

The Quest for Knowledge

As you look within yourself, you'll find the treasure at the end of the rainbow is truth. When you reach true enlightenment, you discover what you've always known. You find that knowledge begins with your truth. You find that death is not the end, but rather a new beginning—a rebirth of your soul into a higher level of awareness.

The pursuit of knowledge is an eternal quest. Your awareness paves the way with understanding. As you continue on your journeys through life, walk with the awareness that your soul, shaped by all that you have been, are now, and will become, is the immortal flame that guides your way.